The Peak District at War

Peter Clowes

To Marion for her patience

ACKNOWLEDGEMENTS

The author is grateful for the help of many people and organisations in the Peak District. In particular he would like to thank Brian Catlin, Alan Watson, Glynn Waite and the Rowsley Assocaition, Alice Hughes, Tony Holmes, the Old House Museum in Bakewell, the Duke of Devonshire and the Chatsworth Settlement Trustees, Stella McGuire, Eric Sharman, Bob Stamper, Dorothy Harrison, Ruth Gordon, Jack Burton, Marjorie Berrisford, Heather Wareing, Chris Sheldon, Frederick Torkington, Clare and John Mortin, and Geoff Fisher.

We shall never Surrender

EVEN though large tracts of Europe and many old and famous states have fallen or may fall into the grip of the Gestapo, and all the odious apparatus of Nazi rule, we shall not flag or fail. We shall go on to the end; we shall fight . . . on the seas and oceans; we shall fight with growing confidence and growing strength in the air; we shall defend our island whatever the cost may be. We shall fight on the beaches ; we shall fight on the landing grounds ; we shall fight in the fields and in the streets; we shall fight in the hills. We shall never surrender.

Extract from Prime Minister's Speech of June 4, 1940.

CHURNET VALLEY BOOKS
6 Stanley Street, Leek, Staffordshire. ST13 5HG 01538 399033
thebookshopleek.co.uk
© Peter Clowes and Churnet Valley Books 2001
ISBN 1 897949 76 6

Foreword

It is now more than 60 years since the last enemy bomber flew over Britain but the Second World War which raged from 1939 to 1945 continues to enthrall students of history and the general public alike. Those who can remember the wintry nights, when the long pencil-thin beams of searchlights swung eerily to and fro over the Peak District, provide vivid insights into the atmosphere of those times.

In this book I have tried to show how the War, with its severe restrictions on civilian life, as well as the perils faced by the armed forces, affected people in the towns and villages of the Peak. The indefatigable spirit of the British people, even in a remote country hamlet like Earl Sterndale where bombs destroyed the local church on the eve of one couple's wedding, induced me to study the effect of the war on these isolated communities. The facts that emerged over the years both surprised and inspired me.

There was the gamekeeper who struggled through snowdrifts to reach an RAF plane that had crashed on Kinder Scout, the schoolboys machine-gunned as they played cricket one summer's evening, the giant decoy town erected on the Derwent moors to confuse German airmen, the air cadets killed on a training flight, the church bells rung to celebrate victory at El Alamein, the vicar taking bottles of beer to colleagues in the Home Guard.

The stories are endless. I hope the vivid pictures in this collection of stories will rekindle graphic memories for some and make younger generations vigilant that such extraordinary times never occur again.

Peter Clowes

Contents

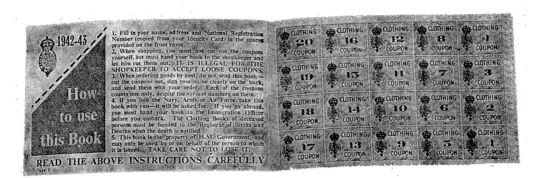

Before the Home Guard was formed posters like this urged older men between 41 and 55 to join Home Defence Battalions. When Anthony Eden announced the formation of Local Defence Volunteers in May 1940 the range was increased to between 17 and 65

Chapter One
Rifles and a Bowler

When icy winds swept over the cottage roofs of Hayfield village and sent smoke from the chimneys whirling and twisting across the slates like skeins of blue wool there was no cosier place than the Club Room at the George Hotel. Here on the top floor of this popular 16th Century hostelry, close to the parish church, a small group of khaki-clad men met every Tuesday night on Home Guard duty during the Second World War. A fire blazed cheerily in a small iron grate. Downstairs in the blacked-out bar beer glasses clinked amid a fug of tobacco smoke as a barmaid made frequent trips up the creaking stairs with tankards of mild and bitter.

"Three men were on regular guard at the George", said Eric Cooper who as an 18-year-old served in the village Home Guard for about 12 months before joining the Royal Fusiliers. *"It was only when we heard the air raid siren that we left that cosy room to walk around the village. It was a much better posting than being sent up to a tiny hut in Ridge Top Quarry on night watch, although from there we had a grand vantage point over all Hayfield and up the valley to Kinder Scout."*

The Home Guard was first known as the LDV (Local Defence Volunteers) and was formed in the dark days of 1940 when Hitler's tanks were racing towards the English Channel and there were serious concerns that Britain might soon be invaded. Anthony Eden, the War Minister, announced the formation of the LDV on May 14th 1940. Any man between the ages of 17 and 65 who had fired a rifle or shotgun and was "capable of free movement" was asked to volunteer. Within weeks 1.5 million men had signed up, nearly half of them veterans of the First World War. The upper age of 65 was only casually observed. Many volunteers were older than 80, the eldest probably being a former regimental sergeant major from Scotland who had originally served in the British Army in Egypt in 1885 - just like the famous character Corporal Jones in the TV comedy series Dad's Army.

Each man was expected to serve for ten hours each week and in the earliest days was given a palliasse, a ground sheet and three blankets. Weapons were difficult to come by. They ranged from broom handles, crowbars and truncheons to Crimean muskets, but after an appeal over the BBC thousands of shotguns and pistols were handed over to the Home Guard. Then a consignment of American and Canadian rifles, which had been in store since 1918, arrived in Britain.

"These Canadian Ross rifles that were issued to us were a bit heavy and thick with grease," said John Duckworth who joined a New Mills platoon in 1940. *"It took us hours and hours to get the things suitable for firing. Then we managed to get our hands on some Short Lee Enfields which were much better."* Jim Drury, who served with the Birchover and Stanton-in-Peak platoon, recalled that they were issued with six Ross rifles and *"they had a kick like a horse"*.

Top priority for Britain's Home Guard was the protection of arms factories and railway lines and the establishment of road blocks in case the Germans landed. Oil barrels, or even old lorries, could be filled with concrete and rolled across open fields where troop-carrying planes might land, or used to block roads. From inside hastily-built concrete pillboxes at road junctions Home Guardsmen could shoot their rifles or hurl "Molotov cocktails" (petrol-filled bottles fitted with match-lighted fuses) at enemy tanks or approaching troops. That was the theory.

The Hayfield company was commanded by Captain Frank Hoyle, a tall, smart, inmaculately-uniformed man who was assistant manager of the District Bank in New Mills. His drill sergeant, Jack Ratcliffe, worked at the Ferodo brake linings factory in nearby Chapel-en-le-Frith, and another sergeant was Fred Gould, a big, brawny man who was a gamekeeper at the Park Hall estate.

The guardsmen drilled each Sunday morning on the church school playground in Wood Lane but what the men enjoyed most was taking part in exercises and mock battles.

"I well remember the Battle of Hayfield," said Eric Cooper. *"Two New Mills companies were ordered to attack Clough Mill which then contained Ministry of Food supplies. But when the invading force began crawling across the fields of Ivy Farm in Little Hayfield Charlie Hobson was furious and ordered them off his land. A red-faced sergeant stood up and refused to go. This was a military exercise, he said. Charlie opened a shippon door and brought out his Dairy Shorthorn bull. That did it. The Home Guard got to their feet and ran. Charlie certainly won the Battle of Hayfield for us."*

Once a month the platoons marched to Bethel Quarry in Valley Road and fired their .303 rifles on a hastily-improvised shooting range.

If any member of the Home Guard failed to report for duty without an adequate excuse he was put "on a charge". Mr Cooper went on, *"I was once sent to New Mills to see Major James Cochrane, the OC of C Company. But I had a good excuse. My night shift at work had prevented me turning up on parade and I was let off."*

Lorries owned by local firms, including the CPA at Strines, were often used to transport Home Guardsmen to remote sites. At Gowhole railway sidings near New Mills six men were housed each night in a camping coach and instructed to watch out for saboteurs as coal wagons were shunted backwards and forwards under shielded lights. Other guardsmen were posted at the local Newtown, Birch Vale and Furness Vale railway stations. *"We stood there, holding our rifles and tried to look important as train passengers walked by on the darkened platforms,"* said John Duckworth. *"I laugh today at Dad's Army on TV, but in the 1940s we took our duties very seriously."*

Occasional escapes by German prisoners-of-war - their camps were scattered

The George Inn at Hayfield. The Home Guard met each week in the pub's club room on the first floor. "Three men were on regular guard here". (Eric Cooper)

A Home Guard patrol and its wartime transport. Vans like this were loaned to volunteer soldiers, as in the Hope Valley by Hancocks, a firm of grocers

across the country - put all Home Guard units on the alert. The most notorious escapee was Oberleutnant Franz von Werra, a German fighter pilot who achieved a considerable reputation after the war as "the one that got away." He and four colleagues dug a tunnel under a barbed-wire fence surrounding PoW Camp 13 at Hayes Hall near Swanwick in south Derbyshire and slipped away during an air raid on a winter's night in 1940.

Von Werra, posing as a Dutch pilot, managed to climb into the cockpit of a top secret Hurricane fighter at Hucknall RAF base near Nottingham where experiments were carried out on high-performance Rolls-Royce aero engines. But his ingenuity was not enough on this occasion. He was arrested after trying to start the Hurricane and sent to a PoW camp in Canada from which, yet again, he escaped, crossing the United States to reach neutral Mexico and eventually returning to Germany in April 1941.

Two of the Luftwaffe men who escaped from Swanwick with von Werra were swiftly recaptured but the other two travelled north to Sheffield, then caught a bus that carried them across the Peak District to Manchester. They arrived on December 24th, one day after the city's "Christmas blitz" and everything was in chaos. They pretended to be Poles and hitched a lift on a lorry travelling southeast back towards the Peak. Two British soldiers were also picked up by the driver and they became extremely suspicious of the two Germans.

By now the Home Guard - at New Mills and elsewhere throughout Derbyshire - were stopping vehicles and carefully scrutinising all identity cards. In the village of Mottram in Longdendale the two Germans were handed over to the police and taken back into custody.

There were escape alerts later in the war for New Mills Home Guard. Two sentries at Gowhole were ordered to stay on duty all night in March 1942 when a couple of German prisoners escaped from a PoW camp at Sudbury in Derbyshire. "Exercise vigilance" was the order. The alert continued for several days and on March 26th the corporal in charge at Gowhole was warned to "take every precaution" - checking empty coal wagons and cattle trucks - as the PoWs were "still at large."

Road blocks were established some weeks later when three Italian prisoners were reported to have escaped from No.11 Camp. They were all young 20 year-olds, one dressed in civilian clothing or brown battledress and one in naval uniform. Drivers of cars and pedestrians were stopped and asked to show their identity cards but there was no sign of the Italians in the Peak District. They were, however, eventually recaptured elsewhere.

Typical entries in the Occurrence Book of New Mills Home Guard in 1941 and 1942, by which time the invasion scare was receding, include the following:

"Ammunition check by Sergeant Maine (three boxes of 60 rounds, one box of 50

Road check-points were enthusiastically set up by the Home Guard during exercises. This North Derbyshire unit is seen on duty on an icy morning in 1941. In the event of invasion concrete-filled barrels were to be rolled across this road.

rounds).

"Town Hall guard provided. Rifles inspected.

Sentry posted.

"Police ask for help in fighting fire on Kinder Scout. Military sending 100 men from Buxton. 55 NCOs and men on parade at 05.45 awaiting transport to Upper House. No arms to be carried, but if possible bring a spade. Eyeshields and respirators required."

On one parade guardsman J.J. Jennison complained that his boots had not been returned by the repairer (Corporal Preece) for nearly three months *"due to a shortage of irons."* On another night no milk was delivered for the sentries' tea. *"Much distress among troops,"* commented Lieutenant Harold Hesketh, the orderly officer. More serious was the absence of several electric torches. *"They appear to have been stolen and this reflects little credit on the Home Guard,"* wrote Captain Jack Henry.

In the early days the men received a subsistence allowance of 1s 6d a night when on duty but this was later doubled to 3s.

There were some odd aspects of the Home Guard in the Peak. When weapons were scarce a volunteer who lived in Laneside Road, New Mills, built a dummy machine-gun fitted with a football rattle so that the gun made a satisfactory noise

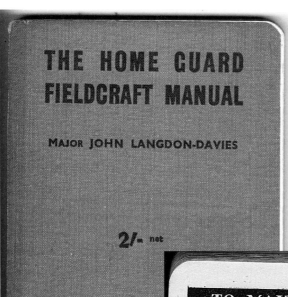

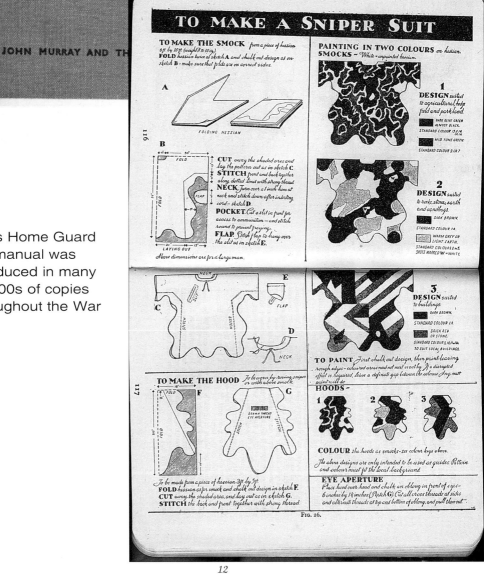

This Home Guard manual was produced in many 1000s of copies throughout the War

during exercises. The town of Buxton, in fact, even had a mounted Home Guard section. The nucleus of the force were farmers who had been cavalrymen in the First World War. Mock charges took place in the woods of Brown Edge and on the slopes of Corbar Hill but their inclusion in the local Home Guard force was more to do with equestrian enthusiasm than being a realistic anti-invasion measure.

The Druid Inn at Birchover. In 1940 the landlord was in the Home Guard and often tucked a bottle of whisky inside his tunic - and on cold nights his colleagues always kept close to him.

Nevertheless, Jim Drury of Birchover remembered the cavalry attacking them during a night exercise near Buxton. *"We had spent the night in a wood near Wormhill, then found some shelter in a barn,"* he said. One of the Birchover Home Guard was the landlord of the Druid Inn and he had wisely pushed a flask of whisky inside his tunic. *"Several of us kept close to him,"* said Jim. Despite the cavalry attack, however, the 2nd Battalion was unable to save the town. Soon a loudspeaker van appeared to announce that the exercise was over and that Buxton had been "occupied by the enemy."

The defenders of Buxton were less successful than the Home Guard unit at Hope and Castleton who, in December 1940 beat off a three-point attack mounted by the Bradwell, Bamford and Derwent platoons. Two Bradwell sections, led by Sergeant Cheetham Fletcher, used three cars to carry them through Bradwell Dale and Peak Forest to Winnats Farm. They grabbed their rifles and moved stealthily down the rugged Winnats Pass in a vain bid to capture Castleton. Other units approached the village from Bamford and Edale but all failed - the Bradwell men being outwitted and captured by the defenders. *"Nevertheless,"* said Sergeant

Fletcher, *"We had a good day and the weather was fine."*

The Home Guard unit at Baslow set up its headquarters in the old Methodist Chapel at Over End and linked this with a lookout post on Eaglestone Moor. Veterans later recalled that a road block was established at Rock Corner on the Sheffield road. Another obstruction, of concrete blocks, was put across Rowsley Bridge, the 17th Century arched structure over the River Derwent.

In north Derbyshire the 1st, 2nd, 3rd and 15th Derbyshire battalions of the Home Guard were eventually formed from the initial LDV. Colonel E.M. Brooke-Taylor, a Buxton man who like so many of his comrades was a veteran of the First World War, took charge of the LDV force in the High Peak and in August 1940 was present when a crowd of 2,000 gathered on the Silverlands football ground in Buxton to watch the first large-scale parade and an inspection by Brigadier General E.C.W.D. Walthall, commanding officer of all the county's LDVs.

There was an invasion scare one Sunday in July 1940. *"A runner appeared at our door with orders for the manning of all posts,"* said Mrs Stella Davies who lived at Pott Shrigley on the western edge of the Peak. *"My two sons hurriedly donned uniform, seized rifles and departed down the lane. No civilians were allowed on the roads without permits."*

There had been reports of "many parachutists" dropping in Derbyshire and both Home Guard and regular army units were turned out. But the scare lasted only a few hours when it was discovered that the parachutes were bundles of hay that had been picked up by a whirlwind and dropped over a wide area.

The scare alerted the Home Guard force in Chinley and squads of men were rapidly despatched to the busy railway station and the village's two bleachworks. Jim Fox, who was 19 when the war started, served in the Chinley Home Guard until it was disbanded in 1944. *"There were about 300 of us in the area,"* he said. *"They were hard years but we had a lot of funny moments."* The "hay invasion" scare was not one of them, however.

When the first parades in Glossop were held on a football field volunteers were issued with LDV armbands. Some of the men carried shotguns and .22 sporting rifles. Former soldiers were promoted to non-commissioned rank, Captain T. Lanceley named as commanding officer and the British Legion's room at the Town Hall converted into a headquarters.

The area the company was made responsible for covered 36 square miles. Soon 500 men had enrolled and a second company was formed. Forty or 50 men were on duty each night. A roadman's hut was used as an observation post at the highest point of the Snake Pass. Here a First World War corporal who held the Military Medal wore a bowler hat and khaki puttees when on duty with six men - and they had just one miniature rifle between them. A small wooden hut was erected on Coombes Rocks above the village of Charlesworth and another post was established at Hollinworth Head near the Grouse Inn on the Hayfield road.

House-to-house fighting was practised at Lower Blackshaw Farm, and at Melandra Castle the base of the ancient monument's south-west tower was used as a machine-gun post.

In Exercise Peak in 1941 the Home Guard pretended to be German troops - each man wearing a red arm-band - when they attacked Glossop, and in the larger-scale Exercise Cotton in October that year scores of army vehicles including tanks, Bren-gun carriers and armoured cars drove in massive convoys over the Peak and along the A624 through Glossop to attack Manchester. Military umpires checked the efforts of all Home Guard units to hold up the attackers and their reports of enemy movements.

It was with pride that the men of the Glossop Home Guard marched in disciplined order on a bright Sunday morning in May 1943. More than 5,700 people gathered in Manor Park to watch and admire their drill.

Some manouevres did inevitably lead to complications. Sidney Wright remembered receiving instructions to attack a farm near Lyme Park. *"We lined up behind a wall on the Bowstones path and a smoke bomb was set off,"* he said. *"The smoke blew back into our faces and we coughed and spluttered and, as a consequence, revealed our presence to the enemy."*

Sidney was ordered to cross the moor and fall as a casualty. *"I tripped,"* he said. *"My rifle went one way, my steel helmet another and my false teeth yet another. Then an officer walked up and said the farm had been captured. We were*

Every village of any size had its Home Guard and Peak towns like Leek, Buxton and Bakewell had many platoons, often based on work places. Here part of the Leek LMS Railway Station Home Guard pose for the camera

all given sal volatile to recover from the effects of the smoke."

The Home Guard at Whaley Bridge carried out manoevres on Taxal Moor - the officers sending messages by motor-cycle despatch rider on the many occasions that field telephones failed to work - and on one extensive exercise, when troops of the Pioneer Corps from Buxton were sent to attack the village, there was much confusion in the Home Guard's Market Street battle HQ. An officer told several young women typists, possibly with his tongue in his cheek, that they would have to evacuate the building down ropes from a rear window. Instead, the horrified girls took to their heels through the front door. *"Then a whistle sounded,"* said one of them, *"And we all went home for lunch."*

During exercises on Stanton Moor one member of the Home Guard tripped over his bayonet scabbard and rolled down a steep slope. *"He was in full equipment with rifle, bayonet, tin hat, gas mask and water bottle,"* said a colleague. *"The noise was deafening."*

New weapons began to reach Home Guard units in the Peak during 1941, the first being the portable anti-tank Blacker Bombard which fired bombs weighing 14 or 28 lbs and was often sited in a trench at the side of roads where enemy armour might appear. The deep trenches could be hazardous. One was dug near Caudwell's Mill at Rowsley and a farmer's horse which fell into it had to be hauled out by the fire service.

The Northover Projector, a similar but more effective weapon, consisted of a long steel pipe mounted on a tripod that fired bottles of phosphorus to ignite enemy

The first commander of Hathersage Home Guard was Captain Schorah. Here, wearing civilian clothes, he watches his unit parade in Station Road, 1940

The Hathersage Home Guard march over Leadmill Bridge in 1940.

tanks. Experts described it as a "graceless" weapon that had to be handled carefully. On one Sunday morning in July 1943 an army officer gave a demonstration in a disused quarry on Beeley Moor to men of the Birchover and Stanton Home Guard. Something went wrong, however, when the Projector was fired. Its bottle of phosphorus zoomed high over the face of the quarry, exploded and set fire to the dry heather. Firemen from Matlock and Chesterfield were called to the scene but it was 10 pm before the widespread blaze was extinguished.

Railway stations were favourite targets for invasion practices. The Bamford unit of the 15th Battalion, Derbyshire Home Guard, under the command of Captain R.W.S. Thompson, a water engineer, was once ordered to attack Hathersage Station, two umpires checking the unit's performance. Unfortunately for the Bamford men, who were lying out of sight behind a wall close to the station, they mistook a whistle blown by the station master for the "end of exercise" signal and revealed themselves to the enemy.

Another "sham attack" on Hathersage occurred in July 1941 when eleven Home Guardsmen from the Bradwell platoon set out down Bretton Clough at 8.40pm on a wet night. *"We all got thoroughly drenched,"* said Sergeant Fletcher, *"And when we reached Hathersage there was no sign of the defenders."* The Hathersage commander had stood down his men due to the bad weather.

Many local Home Guardsmen were employees of the Derwent Valley Water Board who at that time were building Ladybower Reservoir. A small wooden

In December 1944 the Home Guard was officially stood down. Here the men of the
Hathersage unit, many wearing warm greatcoats, pose for a final photograph

observation hut was placed on the moors overlooking Howden Reservoir and at the
end of their period of winter night duty the men were only too glad to be served
bacon and eggs by Mrs Froggatt, wife of the Howden Dam keeper, in her warm
kitchen at Marebottom Cottage in the valley below. Other posts were established on
Crook Hill, the Strines moors, Win Hill and at Crawshaw Head above Moscar. After
maintaining a lookout all night the men were often required to start their normal

Platoons of Leek Home Guard marching through the town

civilian jobs at 8.00am.

The 15th Battalion's main campsite was in Coplow Dale near Little Hucklow, but lorries and vans thoughtfully provided by Hancocks, a local firm of grocers, and the Derwent Valley Water Board avoided many a long march for the men. Rifle ranges were established at Yorkshire Bridge near Bamford and at Edale, and hand grenade practice took place at Bole Hill Quarry near Grindleford. Another quarry, owned by Taylor Frith, was used by the Dove Holes Home Guard for much of the war.

Despite the problems of petrol rationing a local coach was made available for the Bradwell Home Guard when they needed to practise on the Edale rifle range. This duty was much more popular than climbing to observation posts on bleak Win Hill or Mam Tor at five in the morning.

In 1941 a new post was established in a stone building on the edge of Bradwell Moor and here the men on duty could be reasonably comfortable. On May 21st, however, a surprise inspection by the commander found only three men there instead of four - and the sentry failed to challenge Lieutenant Fiennes and Sergeant Fletcher. Two bottles of beer were spotted on the floor. *"Mr Fiennes gave the men a good talking to,"* recalled the sergeant.

At Wirksworth men in their sixties were armed with pitchforks when they went on duty in the early days, sometimes being ordered to sit up in trees to guard a wireworks at Ambergate. When firearms were issued in the later months of 1940 Sunday mornings were set aside for target practice in Middle Peak Quarry and this was much more popular.

One of the Wirksworth unit's lieutenants was the manager of Hunter's grocery store Mr Harold Hodnett who, like all the other part-time soldiers, took his duties

Onecote school - now the village hall - was used as the headquarters of the local Home Guard in 1941. The platoon commander was the Rev W. Campbell

Members of Onecote Home Guard held drill parades in a field at the side of the Green Man
at Bottom House, at first using broomsticks as rifles

very seriously with regular exercises, drill parades and rifle practices. The town
dentist, Mr Arthur Woodward, was also in the unit.

The formation of a Home Guard unit at Onecote in the Staffordshire district of
the Peak was quite an informal affair. The vicar, the Reverend W. Campbell, was
appointed platoon commander and farmer Harold Boulton made a sergeant; Tom
Birch's Austin Seven carried the men to the public house at Bottom House on the
main Leek to Ashbourne road for training with broomsticks. *Then we managed to
get a rifle between us,* said Jim Chadwick, *And our meetings were transferred to
Onecote School. We often marched along Ipstones Road.*

Much of our guard duty was done at High Cross, sitting in Tom Birch's car,
said Mr Chadwick. *The vicar sometimes brought us a bottle of beer.* Manouevres
were held around Grindon and Butterton, rifle practice took place in a quarry on
Caldon Low and the men attended church parades at Wetton Church.

Church parades at Bakewell could be tiring, perspiring affairs. All Saints
Church's situation meant a stiff climb from The Square. Among the men on church
parade was 45-year-old Corporal Joe Mansfield, the manager of Wallis's, an
ironmonger's shop in Bakewell. This popular character was a veteran and hero of
the First World War and had been awarded the Military Medal for his bravery during
a battle in Salonika in 1917. He was one of only a handful of troopers of the
Derbyshire Yeomanry to survive after being surrounded by overwhelming numbers
of enemy infantry.

Many members of the Friden Home Guard were employees of the Derbyshire
Silica Fire Brick company and, under their commander Mr N.A. Lloyd, created an

HQ in the works canteen close to the Buxton-Ashbourne main road at Newhaven. Their main responsibility was protection of the sand-bagged works but they also stood guard at level-crossings over the Bakewell and Cromford roads when trains trundled past on the old High Peak line,

Sundays in 1941 and 1942 were used for the viewing of special instructional films produced by the Ministry of Information. In various villages cinemas such as the Pavilion in Castleton or the Empress in Chapel-en-le-Frith would be opened free of charge so that Home Guardsmen could be shown in graphic detail how to "dismount" enemy motor-cyclists by stringing thin wires across rural roads, how to camouflage themselves with pieces of coloured rag and sprigs of heather and how to conduct guerilla warfare amid the houses of village streets. By this means the ugly reality of war was brought home to the men who had volunteered so enthusiastically to defend their Peak District homes against invasion.

By 1944, however, it was all over. The Home Guard was disbanded and the uniforms and weapons handed in. For many men it had meant discomfort and considerable inconvenience but most of them looked back on their experiences with a certain amount of pleasure - and a great deal of pride.

Probably the Longnor Home Guard, seen outside the Butcher's Arms at Reapsmoor up on the Staffordshire moorlands

Butter Market Home Guard in Leek, No 7 Platoon, B Company 5th Staffs (Leek). Nov 5 1944
Back: S Lovatt E Bratt J Massey J Moss J Hulme F Hulme R Serrell
Middle: W Dykes J Steele A Broadhurst H Campion E Birch B Rabone
Front: E Beech H Fernyhough L Armitt A Whiston J Clowes W Serrell

The Grindon and Butterton Home Guard with a trophy, Cup 194, outside Butterton Church.
There were many cup competitions between Home Guards

Two phographs of the combined Home Guards in Leek, the first showing the men before rifles were generally issued and the second showing a now armed body

Hundreds of girls from Westcliff High School in Southend arrive at Chapel-en-le-Frith Station in June 1940 and head for their new homes in the Derbyshire town. A fleet of buses waits to take other children to nearby villages

Chapter Two
Belles at the Hall

When the evening train from Derby came to a halt in the little station of Chapel-en-le-Frith in June 1940 about 500 teenage girls tumbled out on to the platform. For eight hours they had been travelling from their homes in Essex and they were about to start two of the most unusual years of their young lives.

The battle raging around Dunkirk was at its height. For several days the girls of Westcliff High School in Southend had heard the thud and crump of gunfire and falling bombs as German planes attacked ships in the Thames Estuary.

The local education authority, realising that Southend could soon be in the front line if an invasion occurred, acted swiftly. Parents were notified that nearly 2,000 school children were to be evacuated immediately to the North of England, and on June 2nd the girls of Westcliff High, in navy-brimmed hats, pale blue cotton frocks and white ankle socks, all carrying gas masks in cardboard boxes, gathered in an anxious crowd at Southend Station with their teachers.

When they reached Chapel-en-le-Frith they were met by members of the Women's Voluntary Service and the St John Ambulance Brigade and given refreshments at long trestle tables hastily erected in the Constitutional Hall and the nearby Methodist Church.

It was only 24 hours earlier that a telegram had notified council officials in Derbyshire that the girls were on their way. A survey was carried out and householders were asked to respond to an urgent appeal for billets. A fleet of special buses toured the district and well before midnight on June 2nd all the girls had been found accommodation in Chapel and the surrounding area.

The impact of such a large influx of strangers on a quiet little community amid the Peak District hills was considerable. The vicar of Chapel, the Rev. W.H. Green, organised a "billeting officers' committee". More than 80 girls - inevitably nicknamed "the blue belles" - were found homes at Whitestones, a large country house on the Manchester road formerly owned by a Lancashire cotton baron, which became a temporary hostel. Many villagers offered rooms for single evacuees. Some managed to take in two or three. A hundred girls were sent to Chinley, 50 to Dove Holes and the rest to Peak Dale and the Hope Valley.

Miss D.H. Wilkinson, headmistress of Westcliff High, faced numerous problems. For a month after the school's arrival in Chapel the girls had to be given a holiday as no premises were yet available for their lessons. None of their desks or other pieces of equipment had arrived from Southend.

It was thought desirable to relieve the foster parents of their new charges during the day as much as possible. *"Luckily, the weather was excellent,"* recalled

Teachers took the girls of Westcliff High on long walks in the Peak District until their new school was ready. This party here was in the hills above Combs

Miss Alice Hughes, the school's head of maths. *"We gathered every morning and each teacher took a party on long walks through the countryside, visiting the caves at Castleton, climbing the hills, picnicking in the fields. The Peak District was so new to us. When we returned the girls to their billets in the evening they were tired out - and so were we!"*

Younger children than the teenage girls of Westcliff High had been evacuated from Britain's cities at the very beginning of the war in 1939. In three days nearly one and a half million people were herded on to trains and despatched to unfamiliar areas of the West Country, Wales, the Scottish Highlands and the Midlands and North of England. Nearly a million were primary school children, others were mothers and children under school age going together, expectant mothers, handicapped people and teachers and helpers.

Heavily-pregnant women were evacuated from London and other cities in the south and some had their babies born in Wirksworth Cottage Hospital. Other mothers from the East End of London moved into Willersley Castle at Cromford.

At Lyme Hall Lady Newton converted the Long Gallery of the historic mansion into a war nursery for very young children from London. The billiard table was covered in heavy cloth and the nursing staff slept in rooms off the Knights' Passage. Mr Herbert Rutter, who was employed on the Lyme estate, recalled seeing

Thousands of younger children were evacuated into the countryside at the outbreak of war. This was a typical scene at the main railway stations.

Seventeenth-century Derwent Hall, now submerged under the waters of Ladybower Reservoir, housed 170 girls from Notre Dame School in Sheffield from September 1939 until July 1941. The headmistress complained that the rooms were "unbearably dirty."

Soon after war was declared historic Lyme Hall in Disley, Cheshire, home of the Legh family, was converted into a war nursery for young children from London.

the children being taken on walks through the vegetable garden and picking snowdrops during the winter.

At Stanton in Peak a school from Manchester was accommodated in village homes, the local school on its steep hillside becoming so crowded that Stanton children received lessons in the mornings and the newcomers were taught in the afternoons. Some evacuated children attended the village school in nearby Birchover, the vicar's wife, Mrs Summerfield, taking responsibility for placing them in foster homes.

The parents of girls attending Notre Dame School in Sheffield held a meeting in August 1939 and agreed with the school's governors that some of their daughters should be evacuated to Derwent Hall, a 17th Century building near Ashopton that had been in use as a youth hostel but was now awaiting demolition and immersion in the waters of the future Ladybower Reservoir. The first 170 children arrived there in the first week of September.

The girls were thrilled at the ivy-covered walls of the old building but the nuns of the teaching staff faced many difficulties. A boiler had to be installed to provide hot water and the headmistress complained that the rooms were *"unbearably dirty"* and the artificial light *"appalling"*.

Another pre-war youth hostel, Overton Hall near Ashover, was taken over for 130 boys of Derby School who were accompanied by their headmaster Mr Tom

York. Here the boys slept on bunk-beds and faced the daily chores of washing-up and *"spud-bashing"*. Some of the luckier ones were billeted in nearby farms and houses.

But in June 1940 the school moved to better quarters a few miles away at Amber Valley Camp near Woolley. Some lessons were given in the local Methodist chapel, history and English being taught in a room at the Napoleon's Home public house.

That first day of September in 1939 was a busy time for the teaching staff of many city schools, not least for Mr James C. Burnett, headmaster of North Manchester High School, and his colleagues. They supervised the embarking of 500 boys to new homes in the Peak District. Half the lads went to New Mills and Whaley Bridge, the other half to Bakewell.

The boys, issued with sandwiches, cakes and Thermos flasks for their rail journey and carrying hand luggage in one hand and cardboard-cased gas masks in the other, stumbled out of a train at Bakewell and were greeted by friendly ladies of the Women' s Voluntary Service who handed them buns and mugs of milk from trestle tables that had been erected in the station yard. Mr Burnett marched his lads to Bath Street School where they were assigned to homes in the town by the billeting officer Mr Richard Cockerton, a local solicitor.

The citizens of Bakewell responded to urgent requests to take in the Manchester boys and all had been found accommodation by 8pm. Many accepted more than one boy. The Reverend Henry Sherlock, who had recently retired as vicar of Ashford-in-the-Water, lived in a pretty cottage near the Wye bridge with his elderly housekeeper Miss Astbury. He took charge of two boys and then accepted one of the school's masters, his wife and their one year old child as well.

Many pupils from a large primary school in the Chorlton-cum-Hardy district of Manchester arrived at Hassop Station and were taken by Hulley's coaches to Baslow where the village billeting officer took great care to keep families together as much as possible. At St Anne' s School the headmaster, Mr Jack Sheldon, taught the evacuees in the morning and the village children after lunch.

The expected heavy bombing of Britain did not materialise in 1939, however, and within a couple of months a trek back to the cities started, and this accelerated as Christmas approached.

The Government disapproved but they were powerless to stop it. The North Manchester High School for Boys made the decision to reopen their school buildings back in Manchester at the beginning of 1940 and most of the youngsters returned after the Christmas break.

It was the Dunkirk crisis in May 1940 that brought a new and much more vivid awareness of impending danger to people living on or near the coast. Some 200,000 children, including the Westcliff girls, were immediately evacuated from the vulnerable south-east of England. Hotels overlooking beaches were requisitioned, machine-guns mounted on piers and all bathing prohibited.

It was around this time that the first big impact of evacuation hit the Peak District. Until May 1940 the only evacuees seen in some villages were people who had moved from Manchester or Sheffield into the countryside at their own expense, buying or renting country houses or paying for "rooms."

But evacuated children by the thousand were now arriving in bewildered school parties, clutching their gas masks and with identity tickets tied to their coats. Between June 21st and 24th some 29,000 adults and children from the threatened Channel Islands arrived at Portsmouth and Southampton. Most were immediately sent north to billets in Lancashire, Cheshire and Derbyshire. Boys aged between seven and eighteen from Elizabeth College in Guernsey arrived in Great Hucklow, many of them finding accommodation in the village's Unitarian Holiday Camp with their 12 teachers. They were only just in time - a week later German troops occupied the Channel Islands.

In the same month 600 children from Lowestoft on the exposed coast of East Anglia arrived in Glossop and its neighbouring villages of Hadfield and Padfield. A vast number of children, perhaps as many as 2,000, were also evacuated from Manchester into the nearby sheltering hills.

Bank Hall, a mansion near Chapel-en-le-Frith and once the home of Squire Frith, became the evacuated school for girls of Westcliff High. At the height of summer in 1941 the younger girls practised PT on the lawn.

The headmistress of Westcliff High School moved into Bank Hall, Chapel-en-le-Frith, a large mansion perched in extensive tree-filled grounds on a hillside under the rocks of Castle Naze. It was built in the 17th Century and during Georgian times was occupied by a famous local character known as Squire Frith who hunted foxes on Combs Moss with a pack of ferocious hounds.

Desks, books and sports equipment began to arrive at the hall from the south. Miss Wilkinson and a working party of teachers converted several of the rambling high-ceilinged rooms into classrooms, criss-crossing the windows with sticky tape to protect them against bomb-blast. The bathroom, with its claw-footed iron bath and rumbling hot-water pipes, became the Staff Room.

In July the girls turned up at the hall for their first lessons and, with a revised timetable, examinations for School and Higher School Certificates took place. Surprisingly, despite all the upheaval, *"the results were excellent,"* said Miss Wilkinson.

A second large house, Frith Knoll, became available for first and second-year girls. But it lay two miles from Bank Hall and teachers were constantly changing from one building to the other, carrying books and apparatus with them. A room at Bank Hall was equipped as a temporary science laboratory but sixth-form girls travelled five miles to Buxton twice a week for practical work in the lab of Cavendish High School.

A vegetable garden was established beyond the close-cropped lawns of Bank Hall and 150 girls helped on nearby farms, hoeing and weeding in fields of turnips and potatoes. *"We earned sixpence pocket money,"* said Mrs Dorothy Butcher who also recalled walking the three miles from Chinley to school each day.

Inevitably, there were some difficulties with mischievous girls. Two 14 year olds were billeted with Mrs Lilian Bennett in Chinley. *"I was allowed 5s 6d a week for each girl,"* she said, *"but I gave them a full share of my family's rations. One day I discovered what they had been up to. They would arrive from school before I got back from work, lock out my little boy, then raid the larder to make sandwiches. In the evening they would arrive back from the cinema at Chapel and go straight to their bedroom for a secret supper. Later I accidentally discovered a drawer crammed with food, all of which was rationed, and I was furious."*

The girls evacuated to prestiguous Chatsworth earlier in the war were in a rather different category. They were pupils from the well-known boarding school Penrhos College in Colwyn Bay and in September 1939, when the Ministry of Food took over their buildings in North Wales, they were moved to Derbyshire. About 250 scholars and 36 staff lived at the Duke of Devonshire's home throughout the war years with their benevolent headmistress Miss Constance Smith. The Duke had decided, very sensibly, that a girls' school would make "better tenants than soldiers."

Twenty girls of Penrhos College, Colwyn Bay, slept in the State Drawing Room at Chatsworth House. This painting by Edward Halliday is entitled *Chatsworth in Wartime, 1939*

Numerous chairs and wardrobes, and as many as 26 pianos, were transported from Wales in 30 lorries provided by the Ministry. Part of Chatsworth's splendid library was used for music lessons and the Painted Hall became the school's assembly hall and chapel. Valuable furniture, carpets and other treasures were removed and placed in store as rooms were converted into dormitories. Thirty two girls slept in the large Dining Room, the Orangery became the art room.

The girls were excited by their surroundings. *"One bathroom had mirrors all round the walls,"* remembered one girl. *"Another had its bath sunk in the floor and yet another bath was so big that six girls at a time could get into it!"* On cold evenings some girls fried sausages on the fire in the elegant Stag Parlour. On Sunday mornings the girls walked in long orderly crocodiles to the church in Edensor village a mile away.

While all this was going on the Duke and Duchess of Devonshire and their family lived at Churchdale Hall, a few miles from Chatsworth in the village of Ashford-in-the-Water.

The girls of Penrhos College leave Edensor Church on a Sunday morning and prepare to walk across the park to Chatsworth House. The Duke of Devonshire had decided that the girls would make *"better tenants than soldiers"*

Children from the South of England sometimes had difficulty understanding the Derbyshire accents they encountered. When David Lane arrived at Chinley Station with a school party from Southend in 1940 he was baffled by the shouts of a porter. *"We thought we must be in a foreign country,"* he said. Before attending Hague Bar School in New Mills the children received lessons that hot summer in a field close to a railway line. *"We saw trains with dog-tired soldiers leaning out of the carriage windows. They were coming home from Dunkirk."* In fact, many of these war-weary soldiers were on their way to Ladysmith Barracks in Ashton-under-Lyne where they would recuperate for a few days after their ordeal in France.

One day there was a party for the evacuees at New Mills Town Hall, and Mr Lane remembered the local Swizzels toffee-making firm kindly providing each child with a bag of sweets. In January 1944 a vast New Year's party for 775 evacuees was given by the British Legion in the Victoria Hall at Glossop.

Another school from Southend, St Bernard's Convent, evacuated 500 girls to the New Mills area. They shared facilities with the small town's grammar school - the girls attending classes during the mornings and the local children the afternoons, each school reversing the procedure each term. *"When we were on the early shift it meant getting up at 6am,"* said one convent teacher. *"We had to be clear of the school buildings by 1pm when the other children began to arrive."*

"Sometimes air-raid sirens would wail and everyone trooped off to a line of steel shelters at the side of the sports field in Church Lane. They were half-buried in the ground and contained rows of damp wooden benches. There were usually large pools of muddy water on the concrete floor. Luckily, however, these daylight alerts did not usually last long."

After their school buildings had been damaged by bombs, 50 younger boys from Chetham' s Bluecoat School in Manchester moved to Bank Hall at Chapel-en-le-Frith late in 1942 - the girls of Westcliff High having now returned to their Essex homes. One of the pupils, Alan Hayward, who was billeted at Greendale Farm in Whaley Bridge, recalled: *"The only time we got away from Bank Hall was when we marched down to Chapel Church on Sunday mornings or on one Friday in a month when we were allowed into the town to spend our sweet ration."*

In the years that followed the Second World War many evacuees, now with their own children or grandchildren, have revisited the homes that sheltered them during their young impressionable years. Their memories of the Peak District have invariably been happy ones.

Child evacuees from London arriving in North Staffordshire in 1939

Chapter Three
Sixpence for a Rivet

Some of the most popular spectacles of the war at home were the special weeks devoted to National Savings in which every person in the community was encouraged to "save for victory."

It all started shortly after the Battle of Britain in 1940. The Spitfire fighter aircraft became the nation's favourite. Small metal badges in the shape of the plane began to appear on suit lapels and women's blouses. Spitfire Funds were started and towns invited to buy a plane for £5,000. *"You can buy a wing for £2,000,"* said the Ministry of Information. Even small children could contribute - sixpence would purchase a rivet.

The scheme was so popular that £13,000,000 was raised by April 1941. Spitfires were all the rage - the Hurricane fighter hardly got a look in. The small village of Hayfield set out to fund the cost of three Spitfires but actually raised enough money for seven - a grand total of £35,000. The people of Leek raised money for a spitfire that was called The Spirit of Leek.

To promote further savings spectacular War Weapons Weeks were organised in May 1941. The armed forces cooperated by putting on impressive displays of their hardware and they were fully supported by the Home Guard and National Fire Service. There was a big procession to start the week in Chapel-en-le-Frith. One excited schoolboy recorded in his diary: *"There was a tank on a heavy carriage, two wireless transmitter vans, a searchlight unit and marching columns of police, firemen and air raid wardens."*

In Chapel Market Place there were displays of model aircraft in shop windows and in the electricity showrooms two splendid models, each about ten feet long, of the battlecruisers HMS Hood and HMS Renown. These had been constructed in wood most meticulously by Herbert Slack of Bagshaw. On the town's recreation ground crowds were attracted by an ARP display showing residents how to deal with incendiary bombs and oil fires, and a tall column looking like a giant thermometer displayed graphically how much the savings total was growing.

Local schools joined the savings drives, scholars encouraging their parents to part with cash for weapons. The girls of Westcliff High, for example, raising £3,700 by the end of the month.

In nearby Glossop another long procession snaked through the town to inaugurate War Weapons Week and in the village of Charlesworth a fancy dress prize was won jointly by two young brothers called Castree who were made up to impersonate Hitler and Mussolini.

The enthusiasm generated by these spectacles raised morale and prompted further events of a similar nature. Warship Week was launched in March 1942. At Chapel the giant Slack models were again on display and Commander E.J. Cook took charge of the week's events.

The people of Buxton were asked to raise £425,000, the residents of Bakewell £170,000. Hayfield adopted the Royal Navy's motor launch No. 131 and communicated with the vessel's commander and crew, the village eventually receiving an Admiralty plaque for their efforts. A wireless and other comforts were sent out to the ship.

A larger ship, the anti-submarine trawler HMS Spaniard, was adopted by New Mills during Warship Week in February 1942 but, regrettably, the vessel sank a few months later when a vast petrol explosion wrecked the harbour of Apapa in Nigeria. The town of Leek raised £175,000 to adopt the submarine HMS Unruly which was based for some time in Malta and sank several enemy ships. Geoff Fisher of Leek, a boy of 12 at the time, remembers his school, the Leek High School, adopting the submarine P 49 - a poetry competition was held on the subject of the vessel - and later in the War, a merchant ship called the Sheaf Crown. The boys sent letters and other goodies to the crews   Bakewell adopted the twin-screw minesweeper HMS Derby, sending cash to buy its crew books, cigarettes and chocolate. The ship was based in the Mediterranean and took part in the invasion of Italy,

Wings for Victory weeks were held in 1943 - Bakewell, for example, being requested to raise £120,000 which the residents were told would buy six Mosquito bombers. The town rallied to the task. Flags and bunting were draped outside shops and houses. A children's poster competition was launched in every school and an impressive parade along Bridge Street and Matlock Street included an Air Training Corps drum and bugle band and members of the RAF and A Company Bakewell Home Guard. Hundreds who gathered to watch were also treated to a Civil Defence display in the Market Place.

The local Auxiliary Fire Service brought their trailer pumps to the reservoir at Whitehall Works in Chinley and gave a dramatic demonstration of hose-power and how they tackled fiercely-burning oil fires.

Salute the Soldier weeks occurred in 1944 but by this time the savings drives were running out of steam as the war neared its end. Other schemes organised alongside the savings promotions, however, continued to rely upon the public's generosity. The New Mills War Relief Fund, for example, operated throughout the war, collecting money and distributing cash, cigarettes and Christmas parcels to service men and women and prisoners of war. Girl packers at the Garrison bleachworks and the local dyeworks devoted much of their time wrapping up the parcels. Every local person serving in the armed forces received a parcel and were most grateful.

Gifts of money, hand-knitted gloves, scarves and balaclavas were regularly despatched to local Servicemen by the Rowsley and District Comforts Fund. And this was typical of so many other villages. The war certainly brought out an excellent spirit of comradeship and goodwill in the Peak.

Salute the Soldier Week was held in Bakewell in 1944 to boost war savings. This was the cover of a programme of events in the district - price 3d.

A rambler came across this wreckage of a wartime fighter aircraft on snow-covered Black Ashop Moor in 1946. Scraps of fuselage and pieces of the plane's engine lie scattered over a wide area.

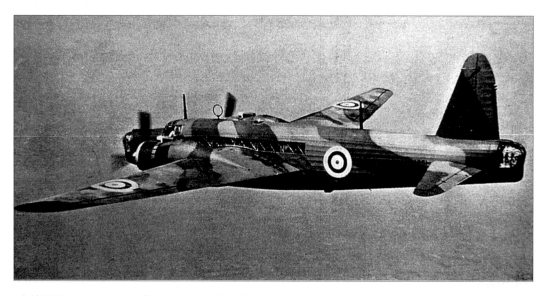

A Wellington bomber. On April 10 1943 Flight Sergeant R.A.Jones attempted an emergency landing on the main Buxton to Ashbourne road at Newhaven. Two men were thrown clear, three others died

Chapter Four
Rescue on the Hills

Thirteen-year-old Hilda Dunn who lived in her father's pub, the Jug and Glass at Newhaven, was awakened by a loud crash at 5.30am on April 10th 1943. A lurid red glow could be seen from her bedroom window and she heard her father dash downstairs.

An RAF Wellington bomber flying on a night training exercise from an airfield near Stafford had suddenly developed engine trouble over the Peak. When one engine failed and the other began to run unevenly the pilot, Flight Sergeant R.A. Jones, decided to attempt an emergency landing. In the moonlight he could see a straight section of the A515 Buxton-to-Ashbourne road. It appeared to be clear of traffic so, after lowering the heavy plane's undercarriage, he touched down on the tarmac surface.

Unfortunately, as the Wellington was running to a halt it slewed round and crashed through a limestone wall into a field only 400 yards from the Jug and Glass. The wing fuel tanks were split open and the aircraft immediately burst into flames.

When Hilda's father, Clifford Dunn, reached the scene with another local man, Tom Rowarth, it was too late to rescue three of the Wellington's crew who had died in the flames. Luckily, the wireless operator, Flight Sergeant R.J. Perrin, and the rear gunner, 23-year-old Flight Sergeant John Douglas, had been thrown clear. The rear gun turret catapulted from the bomber and rolled across the field, Douglas escaping with remarkably few injuries.

Hilda was helping her mother to collect blankets and brew tea when her father and several other men helped the two surviving airmen into the inn. Douglas lay down on Hilda's bed until an ambulance arrived. Buxton ambulance driver Ted Parker said later: "When we got to Newhaven the field seemed full of farmers wandering around with storm lamps. The two airmen we were looking for were in the pub drinking tea - and we joined them for a cuppa."

During six years of war scores of planes came to grief in the Peak District. In many cases airmen had miraculous escapes like the two sergeants at Newhaven.

None could have been luckier than the six men on board a Wellington that set out to bomb U-boat bases at St Nazaire in January 1943. The flight back to their home airfield in County Durham took seven hours and the plane was running low on fuel when it crossed the Pennines. The pilot, Carl Taylor, descended slowly in dense cloud. Suddenly there was a mighty crash and *"heather and herbage began to come up through the floor,"* said one of the crew. The Wellington had hit the only flat part of Blackden Edge - just missing the jagged rocks of Ringing Roger above the village of Edale - and bounced along for 300 yards before coming to a halt in one piece. The airmen stepped out safely on to the peat, only one being slightly injured.

The rocky edge of Ringing Roger on the Kinder plateau looms over the houses of Edale. The crew of a British bomber escaped miraculously in January 1943 when their plane skimmed through the heather and crash-landed high on the moor

The Nag's Head in Edale. From here rescuers climbed to reach injured airmen marooned in the wreckage of their planes on Kinder Scout

Pilot Officer D. Martin, the plane's navigator, said: *"It was pitch black but we heard a train whistle. Three of us set off through the heather, firing a Very pistol at intervals to light the way. We tripped on rocks and fell into a stream."* They eventually stumbled across a farmhouse in the Edale valley and a party of rescuers immediately climbed the hillside to bring down the plane's two pilots and the injured man.

Lee House Farm at the head of the Edale valley. Walkers sheltering from rain rescued an American pilot who parachuted on to their path in April 1943

Strangely enough it was on the same stretch of moorland, only yards away from the isolated spot where Carl Taylor's Wellington had pancaked in January 1943 that two more airmen had miraculous escapes from death nine months later. This time, however, their ill-fated plane did not bounce to safety - it ploughed on to Blackden Edge at speed and broke up.

Sergeant Jimmy Mack, rear gunner of this Halifax bomber, which was returning from a raid on Frankfort, climbed from his battered turret only to find his pilot, navigator and wireless operator dead in the wreckage and the flight engineer dying from massive internal injuries. Only Mack and the bomb aimer had escaped.

It was 1.30am when Mack set out to descend the rough hillside of Blackden Edge and reach help. But it was not until about noon that rescuers found the wreck, and by this time it was too late to save the dying flight engineer.

Another fortunate airman was American John Coenen. He made a parachute jump from his corkscrewing fighter plane as it plunged downwards in thick cloud over the High Peak in April 1943. Fortunately, hiker Bernard Taylor and a group of fellow walkers were sheltering from heavy rain at Lee House Farm near the head of the Edale valley and heard Coenen's Thunderbolt plane crash into the heather on Horsehill Tor. They ran up the rutted track towards Jacob's Ladder and could see the plane blazing just below the cloud level.

To the hikers' surprise Coenen suddenly appeared in his parachute, gliding down and landing heavily, amazingly enough, right on the path. He was in pain with severe back injuries and the hikers wrenched a nearby gate off its hinges to carry him to the farm. Several of the men hurried two miles down the valley to the Church House Inn and phoned for an ambulance. Lucky John Coenen swiftly recovered and was able to return to his squadron in Norfolk four months later.

Even more lucky were the six crewmen of an RAF Wellington bomber who were returning from an aborted raid on Germany with all their bombs still on board one bitterly cold night in February 1942.

Mr Jack Sayles, a waterworks engineer, and his wife heard shouts at midnight as they stood in the doorway of their home at Barbrook Reservoir on the Sheffield side of Big Moor. Someone was carrying a flash lamp and walking along the grass-covered embankment just above their lonely home. It was Sergeant "Kit" Carson, the bomber's wireless operator. When the plane pancaked on the moor he had crawled out of the wreckage and staggered across the frozen surface of the reservoir to reach help for his comrades.

The Wellington's pilot, many miles off course, had been aiming for their base near Whitby. Why the seven 500-lb bombs on board had failed to explode when the

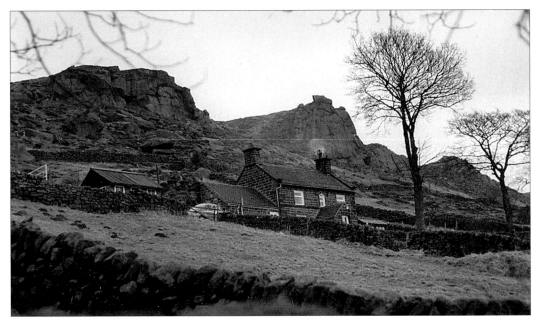

The jagged outcrops of the Roches proved to be a death trap for many wartime aviators. A German JU88 bomber hit by anti-aircraft fire in a raid on Liverpool crashed just below the rocks

plane crashed on to White Edge above the village of Froggatt no one knew. All the airmen were just thankful that they had survived.

Later in 1942 men employed in the dye works at Upper Hulme on the southern edge of the Peak were startled by a low-flying aircraft that emerged out of the mist and just avoided colliding with the mill's tall chimney. A few moments later there was a loud crash when the plane, an RAF Wellington bomber, hit the summit of Hen Cloud in the Roches and burst into flames.

When workmen hurriedly climbed the 1,300-ft high hill they found the plane's rear gunner, Flight Sergeant Samuel Cheek, unconscious with a broken ankle. He had been thrown clear of the wreckage but his five crew mates were dead.

Many more planes crashed at isolated parts of the Peak, including Wildboarclough, Hartington, King Sterndale, Beeley and Black Edge near Buxton, as the war progressed. But the jagged outcrop of dark rocks that form the Roches and lie on the south-west border of the Peak became a formidable death-trap for pilots flying low over the Staffordshire plain.

All the aircraft, except one, that came to grief here were flown by British or Allied crews. The exception was a German Junkers JU 88 bomber, the only enemy plane to come down in the Peak District. This happened in May 1941 after a particularly heavy raid on the Liverpool docks. The plane was hit by an anti-aircraft shell and caught fire. Wireless operator Rudolf Schwalbe sent out a frantic message that the crew were baling out - the pilot was obviously losing control of the plane. At 1am it was seen passing low over the town of Leek with one wing ablaze heading in a northerly direction but before the crew could use their parachutes the bomber crashed on the Roches near Moss End Farm. All four men on board perished.

One of the first local men on the scene was Ernest Bowyer, company quartermaster sergeant of the Leek Home Guard. He and his CO drove up to Royal Cottage, then ran down a moorland lane. *"First we came across a smashed propellor, then a corpse,"* he said. Police and other helpers searched a deep wooded valley as far as Ludchurch before all the German airmen were accounted for.

In fact, another Luftwaffe plane, a Heinkel III, was shot down on the same raid. It crashed at Hazel Grove, near Stockport, only a few miles west of the Peak District, but all the crew were able to parachute to safety and become PoWs.

Many crashes that occurred in the Peak during the war would have been avoidable in later years when nationwide radar and satellite navigation equipment became available. But misjudgements by pilots or faulty navigation often led to planes dropping below a safe altitude in thick cloud and hitting the Pennine hills with fatal consequences.

There was no survivor, for example, when a Swordfish naval plane crashed a few hundred yards from the site of the present-day TV transmitter on Holme Moss in January 1940. It was only when Mr John Davies, a council worker, spotted wreckage while clearing snow on the mountainous Woodhead to Holmfirth road and

The inhospitable edge of Kinder. This is the Downfall. Far below lies Kinder Reservoir which was a useful navigational feature for wartime airmen - nevertheless, many planes came to grief on this rough high plateau.

climbed two miles to the site, that the plane's pilot, Sub Lieutenant Gerald Williamson, was found dead in the cockpit. He had been reported missing four weeks earlier but blizzards sweeping over the Pennines had prevented the wreckage being spotted.

Four airmen died when a Hampden bomber on a training flight crashed on the highest point of 1,730-ft high Rushup Edge, near Chapel-en-le-Frith, in December 1940. A soldier taking an evening's walk on the moors came across the wreckage of an Anson plane that had crashed near the Crowden Tower rocks on Kinder Scout, killing four RAF men, in July 1941. Three Hurricane pilots flying in formation in low cloud died on a hillside above the village of Tintwistle in Longdendale in February 1945. Five American airmen were found dead in the wreckage of their Dakota by a hill walker and his girl friend on Bleaklow in July 1945.

It was on Kinder Scout, at 2,088-ft the highest peak in the district, that some of the most poignant tragedies occurred. The man who knew this wild and desolate area better than anyone was Scottish-born gamekeeper John Watson who lived at Ashes Farm in the fertile valley below Kinder Low. He well remembered one bitterly-cold night in January 1942 when an RAF Hampden bomber flying back from occupied France, with a load of leaflets the crew had been prevented from dropping due to the weather, lost its way and crashed on the moor near Cluther Rocks.

Mr Watson set out to climb the hillside with a storm lantern but was severely handicapped by deep snowdrifts. When he reached the blazing wreckage ammunition was exploding and he could see several bodies amid the flames. He realised he could do nothing to help and it was a very exhausted man who stumbled back to his farmhouse just before dawn. By this time, however, police and airmen had arrived at Ashes Farm. Mrs Watson gave them hot drinks before they set out with a sledge. Late in the afternoon they returned with the bodies of the four airmen who had died.

Mr Harold Hodgson of Hill Houses Farm was one of those who climbed through the snow to reach the plane. *"It was uncanny,"* he said, *"There was deep snow everywhere, yet the whole area was covered with bright leaflets that had scattered from the plane. The leaflets may have been printed in French, I can't remember, but I do wish I had kept one as a souvenir."*

Happily, not all aircraft mishaps in the Peak District ended in tragedy. A young trainee pilot, making one of his first solo flights in a small Tiger Moth, lost his way in 1941 but managed to land successfully in a large field near Rushop House Farm near Sparrowpit. He phoned for assistance, enjoyed a sumptious farmhouse dinner and spent the night in a spare bedroom at the farm. An irate sergeant instructor arrived the following morning, climbed into the cockpit and took off successfully. He then gave a low-level flying display for farmer Alan Virtue and his wife before heading back to an RAF base near Chester.

Two Polish pilots lost their way over the Pennines in 1942 and, with fuel running low in their Tiger Moths, made emergency landings in long grass on a plateau north of Hucklow Edge, one plane tipping over and slightly injuring the pilot. This happened to be the pre-war landing ground of the Derbyshire and Lancashire Gliding Club at Camphill, 1,300-ft above sea level, and the two flyers were lucky to come across it on a day of low cloud and drizzle.

Another Tiger Moth landed in a field near the village of Thorncliffe just north of Leek, a Blenheim light bomber crash-landed in a field near Monyash (ploughing through a stone wall and some overhead wires but the pilot surviving without a scratch), and the pilot of a large American Dakota transport skilfully landed in a field on Ossoms Hill near the Manifold Valley in 1943, several of the crew walking to Wetton Mill and buying cigarettes in a shop at Grindon. They also apparently filled several milk churns with petrol from the damaged plane for the use of villagers. *"Dilute it with paraffin before using it,"* they advised.

Magister training planes made emergency landings at Meerbrook and Cheddleton in 1941, and at Chapel-en-le-Frith one of these two-seat, open-cockpit aircraft came down in a field adjoining Long Lane, one wing striking a tree and spinning the plane to a halt. A local schoolboy seeking souvenirs found a set of dentures on the floor of the cockpit - the pilot having lost them in the rough landing but otherwise escaping with nothing more serious than shock.

Six members of the crew of an RAF bomber which got into difficulties while flying over the Peak District on the night of February 12th 1941 baled out before the plane dived into the ground at Conksbury near Youlgreave. A strong west wind caught the men's parachutes and they fell to earth across a wide area, two landing safely near Over Haddon and others in a field near Sheldon and at Beeley Bridge. Another airman landed in a tree at Swiss Cottage on the Chatsworth Estate (he was comparatively unhurt) and another suffered a sprained ankle when he came down at the side of Park Lane in Rowsley - he was discovered at 8am by a boy cycling to work.

Search and rescue teams in the Peak were organised on a casual basis at first with the police playing a leading part but relying on the invaluable support of skilled hill walkers, men of the RAF, local farmers and village doctors.

But so many planes were coming down in remote and inhospitable areas of the country, such as the Scottish Highlands, Snowdonia and the Peak District, in the early months of the war that an RAF officer at a Welsh base persuaded the Air Ministry to provide special mountain clothing for search and rescue parties consisting of medical orderlies and keen volunteers. Grooved-heeled nailed boots, windproof anoraks, rucsacks and walkie-talkie sets were issued.

In 1943 a permanent Mountain Rescue team was established at Harpur Hill RAF base near Buxton. Already Flight Lieutenant David Crichton, a medical officer at Harpur Hill and an enthusiastic mountaineer, had been training volunteers to cope with rescue missions. The unit was soon being called out to all parts of the Peak and by the time they received official recognition by the Air Ministry they had attended more than 40 crashes. By the end of 1944 the number had risen to 50, with 49 airmen rescued.

Although a Mountain Rescue Committee had been established in the Peak District in the 1930s to deal with walkers who got into difficulties; and posts and equipment centres set up in high-risk areas, the RAF Mountain Rescue service gave an impetus to the efforts of local hill walkers when the war ended. In 1959 rescue teams were established in New Mills and Glossop and the Peak District Mountain Rescue Organisation was formally named five years later. Now there are efficient mountain rescue posts, all manned by volunteers and equipped with Land Rovers, mobile phones and the very latest rescue equipment, throughout the Peak. But most of their call-outs these days deal with falling rock climbers or walkers becoming lost or injuring themselves on the moors.

John Douglas, the airman who survived the Wellington that crashed at Newhaven, travelled from his home in Carlisle to the Jug and Glass Inn in 1982 for a reunion with the girl who gave up her bed for him that eventful night in 1943. Hilda Dunn, now Mrs Kirkham, came from her home in Ashbourne. "I often thought about him over the years," she said, *"It was marvellous to see him once more."*

Aircraft technology has vastly improved and it is now rare for a plane to fly into trouble over the hills of the Peak, but the memories of those dark days of the 1940s are still vivid for many of the people involved.

Chapter Five
A Church in Flames

It was a disconsolate couple who gazed at the smoke-blackened and still-smouldering ruins of St Michael's Church, Earl Sterndale, one crisp morning in January 1941.

William Wain and his young fiancee Annie Harrison were due to be married in the church the following day. Both were from local farming families who had lived in the nearby hamlets of Pomeroy and Brandside for many years and they had been looking forward to a joyous well-attended ceremony in the 120-year-old building.

Then the vicar, the Reverend George Cook, walked up, stepping carefully over a network of fire hoses lying in the frosty grass. He smiled grimly. *"That's the war for you,"* he said, *"But don't worry. We'll go ahead with the service. We'll manage, just you see."* Late the previous night a German plane had dropped a load of incendiary bombs in the fields around the small Derbyshire village and several had struck the church, setting the entire building ablaze.

But at 11 am on Saturday January 11th the wedding service went ahead as the vicar had promised. The church roof had been destroyed, the windows smashed and the flagged floor was a mass of charred woodwork and rubble. Even the Saxon font had been broken into pieces.

The Reverend George Cook, in a white cassock, stood in the ruined chancel in front of twin lancet windows in the east wall as William, wearing a belted overcoat against an icy east wind, and Annie, in her best tweed coat, kneeled before him. At either side of the couple stood their parents. It was a moving open-air ceremony that somehow epitomised the indefatigable spirit of those wartime days.

Mrs Kathleen Nadin, whose husband was in the army, lived at Fernydale Farm in the village and recalled the night of the bombing. *"My infant son was fast asleep in his cot when we heard the sound of a plane,"* she said. *"Then we could smell burning and at first thought that our own farm was on fire."* Soon, however, she and her mother saw flames leaping from a barn at Harley Grange Farm across the fields. Already men from the village pub, the Quiet Woman, were running to help and the fire brigade was summoned from Buxton. Immediately below the barn was a ground-floor shippon. Two cows died and before the rest could be driven to safety two more were badly burned and had to be put down later by a vet.

More incendiary bombs - about 50 it was later estimated - began to splutter and flare in the fields. One fell outside the village shop and 16-year-old William Kidd, who had seen demonstrations given by local air raid wardens, swiftly shovelled soil on to the flames to extinguish them. Another villager said: *"The hills were lit up like Christmas trees."*

The marriage of William Wain and his fiancee Annie Harrison goes ahead amid the wreckage of St Michael's Church, Earl Sterndale, on the morning after bombs had rained down on the small village. Conducting the service is the local vicar, the Rev. George Cook. This picture epitomises the indefatigable spirit of the British people in wartime days

Then the church began to blaze, a bomb having fallen through the slate roof and setting fire to the pews. In the confusion men who ran to the scene could not at first find the door key. This caused some delay and the blaze swiftly spread to the church roof. The fire brigade called to Harley Grange Farm now tackled this fire, but they were too late to save the building. It was the only Derbyshire church to be destroyed by enemy action during the entire war.

Mrs Mary Wheeldon, then a girl of nine, watched the blazing buildings from the doorway of her home at Street House Farm, Pomeroy, about a mile away. *"It was a bitterly cold frosty night and there was bright moonlight for the enemy pilots,"* she said. Another girl, now Mrs A. Gilman, saw the blaze from a window at Hall Farm, Hollinsclough, a village just over the hills to the west. *"We didn't go to bed at all that night,"* she said.

Many people living around Earl Sterndale heard the dull crump of falling high-explosive bombs and it was widely believed that German planes targeted the RAF camp at Harpur Hill, only about a couple of miles away, where there was a large store of bombs. This could be true, but it is more likely that the incendiaries came from planes returning home from raids on North Western cities and ditching bombs they had failed to release on the target areas.

After raids on Manchester or Liverpool - or as far off as Barrow-in Furness or Belfast - surplus bombs were often released at random while the planes flew back to their Luftwaffe bases in Occupied France. Their route frequently lay directly over the Peak District and this could explain so many of the "bomb incidents" reported. In fact, a total of 80 high-explosive bombs fell in the south-eastern area of the Peak during the war.

The high-explosive bombs heard in Earl Sterndale could have been several that were dropped around Buxton that night. A stick of bombs landed in fields near Daisymere Farm at Waterswallows and as late as 1987 the tail fin of an unexploded 500-lb bomb was unearthed in the garden of a house in Fairfield.

When air raids were thought to be imminent - RAF radar having detected bombers crossing the coast and their course then plotted by the Royal Observer Corps - phone calls were made to the police and sirens, often mounted on the roofs of police stations, switched on. Where wailing sirens had not been installed factory hooters were used, sending out a series of short blasts into the night air and causing many people to grab armfuls of blankets before scurrying for shelter under their stairs or in basement areas.

On "Eagle Day", August 13th 1940, the Germans sent a special force of Heinkel bombers over Britain. At 10 pm they arrived over the Peak District and other parts of the Midlands and began scattering large numbers of empty parachutes, and even some radio transmitters and maps, to give the impression that an invasion was imminent. In fact, listeners to Lord Haw-Haw, the German radio propagandist, later heard him falsely claim that parachutists had actually landed in England and were being harboured by Fifth Columnists. Many flares were dropped that night and the hills of the Peak were vividly illuminated before several bombs fell. Two weeks later more bomb explosions echoed around the hills, a string of 19 falling across the Foolow-to-Windmill road near Great Hucklow and slightly damaging a bungalow.

There was a further indiscriminate raid on the night of August 31 when a single high-explosive bomb and a string of incendiaries dropped in fields at the side of Hollinsmoor Road in Rowarth, smashing windows at the Children's Inn and Laneside Farm and shaking whisky bottles from shelves in the Little Mill Inn. A villager making his way home from the Moorfield Arms was thrown to the ground. "There seemed to be millions of candles around me," he said.

Earl Sterndale's parish church in better days. It was the only Derbyshire church to be destroyed by enemy action during the war. A single incendiary bomb falling through the roof and setting fire to pews is thought to have caused the damage

Incendiaries were scattered around Baslow on September 12th, the first parachute mine to be dropped in the Peak fell near Ivanbrook Quarry at Grangemill on October 21st and on the same night at 3.30am several houses were damaged by four bombs that fell at Moorseats in Hathersage. Two bombs exploded west of Eyam on December 20th. Strings of incendiaries also fell between Kempshill Farm and Wormhill, two of the bombs landing in a farmyard, and more were dropped around the village of Brassington.

That winter particularly heavy raids were made on nearby cities, 2,800 homes being demolished in Sheffield on December 12th and 15th, 600 people being killed and 75,000 houses damaged in Manchester on December 22nd and 23rd.

For some time the Ministry of Defence had feared heavy air raids on Britain's cities and a month before the Sheffield blitz troops were sent on to the wild, heather-covered Derwent Edge, which was about eight miles from the city's great steel plants, to build a dummy town on the moors. The "Sheffield decoy" extended for some miles along the ridge and simulated a two-thirds scale row of blast furnaces, two stretches of factory roadway and four marshalling yards. Some bombs did fall on the decoy but, unfortunately, on the nights of the blitz a full moon made the city easily visible to enemy pilots and the blaze of dummy lights on the Peak District

Volunteers in the Royal Observer Corps, usually men over military age, crouched in draughty huts on exposed hill-tops in the Peak to spot enemy bombers through their binoculars. A typical site was the summit of Eccles Pike near Chinley where the Corps' hut was secured by sturdy ropes behind these rocks

moors was only partially effective. A few stray bombs fell into fields at High Lees, Hathersage, but caused no serious damage.

When bombs were raining down on Sheffield the girls of Penrhos College, now at Chatsworth only a few miles from the city, were swiftly assembled in the cellars, packed tightly together on wooden forms. *"Cream crackers and Bovril would eventually be passed down the rows until the all-clear sounded,"* said Nancie Park, then a pupil at the school.

The bomb damage on the night of December 12th was so serious in Sheffield that workmen were despatched from nearby villages to help clear the rubble. Soon after dawn in Baslow, which lies only ten miles from the city, every available man who worked in the building trade was rushed over Big Moor by coach and lorry. Many of them went to repair the roof at the Effingham steelworks.

At New Mills School sturdy steel air raid shelters were erected at the side of the playing fields and half sunk in the ground under two feet of soil. On May 12th 1941 one schoolboy wrote in his diary, *"The siren went at noon while we were having a physics lesson. Prefects threw open the classroom doors and we went into the shelters for 15 minutes, sitting on damp benches with our feet in pools of water."*

Mobile searchlight units were set up at strategic positions throughout the Peak, their pencil-thin beams criss-crossing the sky at night in desperate bids to catch sight of the raiding planes. One unit set up station in remote countryside near Cowburn Tunnel north of Chapel-en-le-Frith and another in Coplow Dale near Little Hucklow. A searchlight set up off Asker Lane, Matlock, was alongside a heavy anti-aircraft gun unit. Heavy guns were also stationed off Moorland Road in Hathersage.

From Stella Davies's farm, 600 feet above Pott Shrigley, there was a "grandstand view" across the Cheshire Plain of the Manchester and Liverpool bitzes. *"Night after night the sky was red with the flare of burning buildings,"* she said. On one night a plane zooming high over the farm buildings dropped a stick of bombs that blasted a silage pit and broke the windows and walls of a nearby cottage - the occupier, Mrs Taylor, and her children being extricated unharmed but shaken. Like so many other schoolboys in Britain, ten year old Ray Booth collected many jagged pieces of shrapnel that he found scattered across the fields around Pott Shrigley.

Another "grandstand" view of the cities receiving their awful pounding was from Flash, south of Buxton and reputed to be the highest village in England. On many nights the Vicar of St Paul's Church, the Reverend Horace Graves, and the local policeman George Gardiner would stand across from the New Inn and look at the distant crimson sky with expressions of horror as German bombers moaned overhead.

A German plane returning from the Manchester blitz on December 23rd 1940 dropped two bombs into a field at Greenhills between Ashford and Bakewell. No one was hurt but many houses on the Lakeside estate had their windows smashed. Incendiaries were dropped around Youlgreave on the same night.

Several bombs were jettisoned over Leek on the night of March 11th 1941, one falling through the roof of a house in Nunn Street and killing 28 year-old baker Albert Carding. Incendiaries were scattered across the town centre. Seventeen year-old Walter Serrell came out of the Majestic Cinema when the air raid siren sounded and with his friend Fred Murfin threw sandbags over some of the blazing bombs .

Nine more bombs crashed down at Nether Water Farm, Little Hucklow, at 10pm on April 7th 1941, badly damaging the barn and other farm buildings, and eleven more bombs fell in fields near Youlgreave yet again on May 7th. Two parachute mines exploded on the slopes of Mam Tor, the Peak District's 1,695 ft "shivering mountain" near Castleton the following night. A few weeks later several small bombs made craters behind the rocks of Cracken Edge at Chinley and incendiaries scattered over the town of Leek set fire to several shops including the Burton's clothing store.

It was on rugged, rock-littered Derwent Edge that a decoy town was built to deceive enemy bombers attacking Sheffield. Nowadays this is a lonely part of the Peak District visited only by ramblers and occasional sheep but in 1940 there were imitation blast furnaces and marshalling yards strung along the moor

Incendiaries fell in Lyme Park near Disley. These evil devices, weighing about 2 lbs each, could be particularly destructive. They did not explode on impact but burned steadily for up to ten minutes sending out magnesium sparks which set fire to everything within a few feet. Margaret Bowden, then a schoolgirl, recalled how she and her father who was employed at Lyme, ran out with sand buckets to extinguish them. Several incendiaries fell around the historic hall but only one landed on the actual buildings. That was the laundry and luckily the bomb failed to ignite.

The inhabitants of Youlgreave thought they were receiving particular attention from the Luftwaffe when yet another shower of incendiaries fell around their homes in December 1942, two of the fire-bombs going through the roofs of cottages in the village. A 12-year-old girl living at Coldwell End saw three fall in the garden. *"My father tried to put them out with a coat but to no avail,"* she said. She and her mother crouched under a table, but were later persuaded to shelter across the road. *"I grabbed my dog under one arm and the budgie cage with my other hand,"* she said. But, apart from a high-explosive bomb falling harmlessly near Dale Farm in Conksbury Lane, there were no more alarms for the excited villagers.

Night after night the sky flickered with the distant red flashes of anti-aircraft fire. This was accompanied by the crack and rumble of bomb explosions, but most people in the Peak managed to sleep through it all.

By the summer of 1942 most of the daylight air raids were being carried out by one or two bombers. Two planes in particular, Junkers JU 88s based in France, caused mayhem in the Peak one mild evening in July of that year. They had set out to make a surprise low-level daylight attack on the De Havilland propellor factory near Bolton. They flew up the Irish Sea and, to avoid anti-aircraft batteries clustered around Merseyside, crossed the coast near Southport. They missed their target, however, and flew on south-eastwards towards Derbyshire.

The villages of New Mills and Hayfield were the last clusters of buildings they came across before reaching the high moorland of the Peak District. At 8pm, as the New Mills Town Hall clock was striking the hour and many people were in the Union Road Cinema watching a Will Hay film, the two planes, flying at little more than 100 feet, appeared over the gas works and opened machine-gun fire on the large gasholder. Bombs fell in the River Goyt and a nearby street, and one of the planes sprayed the local cricket ground with machine-gun bullets - the schoolboys playing a friendly match throwing themselves flat as bullets ripped diagonally across the pitch. Miraculously, all the boys escaped injury.

The little town's chief air raid warden thought the explosions were caused by a road crash, until he saw smoke rising into the evening sky.

Further bombs fell on an iron-roofed Methodist chapel and a house in the Low Leighton district, killing two people, one of them ten-year-old Joan Handford as she played the piano.

The planes flew on up the Sett Valley and swerved over the rooftops of neighbouring village Hayfield, dropping another bomb which demolished cottages in Spring Vale Road and killed six people. They then flew south over Colborne and Old Moor, picking up speed but still flying very low.

Schoolboy David Turner, who was helping the haymaking at First Riley Farm near Eyam, said: *"I was with Mr Johnson on top of the hayrick when we saw the planes sweep across Middleton Dale."* Several incendiary bombs were dropped in Eyam Quarry, not far from the dust-covered cottages of Stoney Middleton, and *"we saw smoke coming up."* Luckily, the incendiaries fell in the bottom of the old quarry, well away from any buildings.

At Chatsworth House the girls of Penrhos College had gathered in the Painted Hall for evening prayers when the words of Miss Edman, the deputy headmistress, were suddenly interrupted by a crash that sounded like someone *"dropping a huge load of crockery."* The two Junkers planes were spraying the house with machine-gun fire. The girls fled to the beer cellar and were unhurt. Luckily, the only damage sustained was a series of holes punched in woollen swimming costumes that had been left outside to dry in the evening sunshine!

The bombers never reached their French base, however. Two Polish pilots took off from an RAF station near Scunthorpe and shot down both planes before they could cross the coast. One plane plunged into farm buildings, killing all the crew, and the other made a forced landing, its crew being captured by members of the Home Guard.

The day after this series of raids a High Peak schoolboy wrote in his diary: *"Heard that New Mills was bombed last night so went to see for myself. When I got off the train I was astonished. Lowe's Mill had most of its windows smashed and the roof of the station signalbox had been ripped into shreds. One bomb appeared to have fallen in the river. Two policemen stood sheltering from the rain in a splintered doorway at the mill. Nearby was a red notice "Unexploded Bomb - Keep Clear. Yet the bomb, a rusty-looking thing, lay in a wheelbarrow. Someone had pulled it out of the river and we were able to walk up to within a few feet of it."*

"Many shop windows in Market Street and Union Road were broken. A notice on one boarded-up window read 'Open as Usual'".

"The house hit in Low Leighton was totally destroyed. Just one corner of the kitchen, containing the back door, was left standing. There were pieces of twisted iron in a field 100 yards away and several bricks that had been hurled across the road were stuck in the slates of the old hospital. Every window was boarded up and tarpaulins draped over large holes in the roof."

A Junkers JU88 light bomber of the Luftwaffe. The crews of two of these planes killed eight people and machine-gunned schoolboy cricketers in New Mills one July evening in 1942

The wreckage of two cottages in Spring Vale Road, Hayfield, where six people were killed during a low-level daylight raid in 1942.

"My friend Norman Handford, whose sister was killed, escaped because he was at an Air Training Corps drill. We saw him today still in his blue uniform, trying to smile but looking ill."

This foray by the Luftwaffe marked the virtual end of the Peak District "blitz." Few more bombs fell amid the moors and dales during the remaining years of war, until a mass "doodle-bug" raid awakened everyone's fears again in 1944.

From June of that year - only a few days after the Allies landed in Normandy - a new weapon, the ingenious ramp-launched V1 flying bomb, had been landing in south-east England in large numbers and causing many casualties.

On Christmas Eve the Germans tried a new tactic by launching 30 "doodle-bugs", as they were called by the British, from Heinkel bombers cruising 40 miles off the east coast between Skegness and Mablethorpe. These early Christmas presents were intended to land in Manchester but the high-speed pilot-less planes, each one crammed with explosives, wandered off track, most coming down north or south of the city. They did, however, kill 40 people. Four "doodle-bugs" plunged into open ground in the Peak District.

Farm workers in Combs, near Chapel-en-le-Frith, arising at 5.30am, saw a red glow from the exhaust of a plane streaking low across the hills. One said the machine made a *"sinister growl"*, other people described it as spluttering *"like an aerial motor-bike"*. The engine suddenly stopped and the plane plunged on to Black Edge on the Dove Holes side of Combs Moss, killing a solitary sheep and creating a vast crater from which a plume of white smoke arose.

Novelist Crichton Porteous, who lived in a bungalow under the looming shoulder of Combs Moss, was awakened like many others by the thunderous crash which shook every house in the village. Alan Virtue at Rushop House Farm, three miles from Combs, felt the stone farmhouse shake, so violent was the explosion. *"My cows started bawling and the horses scattered."* he said.

At about the same time another flying bomb hurtled into the ground in the far west of the Peak District at Macclesfield Forest. Just below the rocky hill known as Tegg's Nose two farms, Crooked Yard and Clough House, narrowly escaped disaster - the "doodle bug" gouging a crater 27 feet deep in a field and ripping much of the roof off Crooked Yard Farm. Schoolboy William Slack was rudely awakened at nearby Five Ashes Farm to find the bedroom window shattered and pieces of glass covering his bed.

Bomb craters in the countryside inevitably attracted the attention of children seeking pieces of shrapnel. A stray German bomb fell in the Seal Field-High Lees area near Sheffield Road in Hathersage in 1940 and left this large crater. In the foreground are the young Spitalhouse brothers and Bob Stamper

The bombers' final target on the evening July 3 1942. The walls of Chatsworth House were sprayed with machine-gun fire and the schoolgirls of Penrhos College fled to the beer cellar

Another flying bomb was reported to have come down at the head of the Goyt Valley on Burbage Edge, only a couple of miles from Buxton, and another to have exploded harmlessly amid heather and outcrops of rock on Midhope Moors near Margery Hill, one of the remotest parts of the Peak high up the Derwent valley.

Although these were the last bomb explosions in the Peak there was one final raid on March 4th 1945 that sent many people in Matlock town centre scurrying for cover. A lone German bomber, probably a JU 88, circled the town two or three times that Sunday morning before opening fire. Several buildings including St Peter's Church were hit by cannon shells but, miraculously, no one was hurt. Local schoolboys had a grand time afterwards picking up spent ammunition in the station goods yard and near Burgon's shop in Crown Square.

By now the war was almost over. Victory in Europe was only a month off and the Peak District could breathe easily once again.

Chapter Six
Blizzards Bury the Barrel

It was not just the irksome difficulties of air raids and rationing that affected people living in the higher parts of Derbyshire. The weather could also make life wearisome and in January 1940 one of the country's most severe snowstorms caused transport and communications problems that almost paralysed the Peak.

The temperature in Buxton fell to -18°, the lowest ever recorded in the town for nearly 50 years. In one week there was a level fall of nearly three feet and drifts as high as 20 feet were recorded.

Roads out of town were blocked by snow that covered the stone walls on either side. Buses were unable to get through. One man, however, managed to clamber over the drifts on a six-mile trek from Chapel-en-le-Frith to Fairfield to attend Hilda Bould's wedding at St Peter's Church, although several other guests including the best man did not make it. And when a North Western bus travelling from the Ferodo works to Buxton was halted by drifts in a raging blizzard at Batham Gate the 23-year old woman conductor, Marjorie Moss, wrapped in a thick coat and balaclava, trudged in front of the vehicle to guide the driver as he reversed back to the Railway Inn at Dove Holes.

Another girl conductor, Elsie Twigg, remembered her bus becoming stuck in a snowdrift on the high road between Chesterfield and Baslow. All the passengers

Severe winter weather in the early months of 1940 brought much of the Peak District to a standstill. This train laden with war supplies became stuck in deep snowdrifts that filled a cutting near Stodhart Bridge, Chapel Milton, on the main Derby to Manchester line. The train's driver, fireman and guard sheltered in a nearby signalbox. The line was blocked for several days

had to struggle on foot back to Baslow, although kind-hearted Mrs Bradbury at Wardlow Wells helped by fortifying them with cups of hot tea.

In some villages no newspapers were delivered for a week. The big quarries at Peak Forest and factories throughout the areas including the printworks at Strines and the bleach works in Birch Vale, were forced to close down temporarily.

There was chaos on the railways, affecting troop trains and goods trains loaded with war supplies. On the night of January 27th a heavy goods train on its way from Trafford Park to Rowsley became derailed on hard-packed snow at the end of Chapel Milton viaduct. For two days the crews of the two locomotives and their guard took it in turns to struggle through deep snow from the shelter of a signalbox to obtain food from a shop in Chinley. All rail routes in the district were disrupted but a relief crew reached the stranded train and allowed the beleagured men to move to the Princes Hotel in Chinley for three days until the line down to Manchester was cleared and they could return to their homes in Rowsley via Crewe and Derby.

Another train of empty coaches became entombed in a cutting only half a mile from Chapel Milton and it was a week before troops from Lancashire were able to dig it out of the giant drifts. Local people brought the cheerful soldiers buckets of strong tea. The last train into Hayfield that Saturday night stayed there for two days, although a light engine managed to break through walls of snow with newspapers for the village before a renewed blizzard cut off the station once again.

The fuel position became desperate as there was only a limited stock of coal in the Hayfield goods yard. Householders in New Mills were similarly affected. Scores bought coke from the local gas works but had to drag the heavy bags up an ice-covered cobbled hill from Mouseley Bottom.

Men employed at mills forced to close down were recruited as "snow-shifters" on the roads. Soldiers of the 2nd Corps Royal Signals, based at Bakewell, turned out to clear the exposed roads on Flagg Moor. A Society of Friends meeting house was converted into a temporary canteen, and the landlord of the isolated Bull i' th' Thorn allowed the troops free access to the inn, although he had limited supplies of beer and the pub soon ran dry!

The Sheffield road from Glossop was completely blocked and prisoners of war worked in relays to load the snow on to lorries. *"It never stopped snowing for three days and nights,"* recalled Mrs Elsie Heywood. *"It kept melting and freezing until it was as hard as marble, and there was even some left at Whitsuntide."*

Harry Stafford of Whaley Bridge, who was given a 48-hour pass by the army to get married, arrived at Stockport Station and obtained a lift for part of the way home. *"The drifts were 15 to 20 feet high,"* he said. Neighbours turned out in force to clear the road for a taxi carrying Harry's bride to reach church the following day.

The Barrel Inn at Bretton was cut off for 12 days. Snow covered all the windows and a tunnel had to be dug through the snow to the door. *"It looked like a huge igloo,"* said one man who trudged along the narrow lane from Eyam.

The picturesque Barrel Inn at Bretton was cut off for 12 days in 1940, a tunnel having to be dug through giant snowdrifts which covered all the front

High winds and heavy encrustations of ice snapped electricity pylons on Tom Thorn near Buxton, food was dragged by sledge to scattered houses around Ashover near Matlock, telephone wires at Flash were coated with ice three inches thick and the local vicar, the Reverend Horace Graves, remembered removing icicles from his ears after walking from his parsonage to St Paul's Church for morning service.

The bitter winter of 1940 brought mixed fortunes for evacuated schools. A wheezing school bus was unable to negotiate the lane that climbs from Chapel-en-le-Frith to Bank Hall. Deep drifts filled the lane from wall to wall. A council snow plough arrived but as swiftly as it cleared a path a howling blizzard filled it in again.

The girls of Westcliff High and their teachers put haversacks on their backs and walked two miles to the hall. Some classes had to be held in the village Constitution Hall. But at Chatsworth, where the famous Cascade and lakes were frozen solid, the girls of Penrhos College sent home requests for skates and enjoyed sliding and toboganning on the ice.

It was not just snow that created havoc in 1940. Heavy and persistent rain in the Pennines during the Whit weekend swelled streams pouring down the steep valleys at the northern tip of the Peak. The normally-placid River Holme that meanders through the town centre of Holmfirth became a raging torrent 18 feet high. Houses in Huddersfield Road, Upperthong Lane and Hollowgate filled with water. Several buildings in Hollowgate and Victoria Street collapsed and some people were trapped in Scar Fold below the "Nora Batty" house later featured in TV's *Last of the Summer Wine*. Three people were drowned and 200 houses were flooded.

The clearing up took several weeks. Better weather lay ahead., but the war, of course, went on.

The great stone towers on the Derwent Reservoir wall made ideal markers for Guy Gibson's "Dambuster" squadron on their practice flights. Gibson himself flew over the dam. The experiences of these gallant airmen led to successful raids on the Mohne and Eder Dams in Germany in May 1943

Chapter Seven
Defending the Dams

The villagers of the Derwent Valley looked up at the sky from the windows and doorways of their cottages and farms one evening in March 1943 when a procession of black-and-green Lancaster bombers roared over the two reservoirs that lay between the steep slopes of the Howden Moors and Birchinlee Pasture.

The planes were flying exceptionally low and crossed the Derwent Reservoir between the turreted towers that stood at the sides of the stone dam wall. *"We thought they were going to crash,"* said Mrs Olive Booth of Ding Bank Farm, Ashopton. *"Then my husband and I decided they were just RAF lads out joy-riding and wasting petrol."*

But the Booths changed their minds some weeks later when they heard news on the radio that RAF bombers had attacked several important dams in Germany and had practised their low-level "bouncing bomb" technique in the Peak District.

Wing Commander Guy Gibson had hand-picked crews for a special Squadron X, later immortally known as 617 Squadron (the Dambusters), to undergo intensive training for the raid. Each Lancaster was to carry an enormous five-ton cylindrical bomb which was to be dropped from a height of only 60 feet. The inventor Barnes Wallis had devised a spinning mechanism that made the bomb skim across the surface of a reservoir and sink alongside the dam wall before exploding. This obviously required a very high standard of flying by the pilots and crews.

The squadron was based at Scampton in Lincolnshire and on March 27th 1943 Flight Lieutenant Bill Astell, a 23-year-old whose home was in the Peak District, was ordered by Gibson to *"fly over every lake you can see in England, Scotland and Wales and take photographs of them."*

On the following days Gibson himself, piloting his favourite Lancaster G for George, headed for various parts of the country where lakes were situated. On May 4th and 9th he flew over the Derwent Reservoir and decided that it would make a perfect practice area for the forthcoming highly-secret attack on the German dams.

"This lake is in the Pennines, surrounded by high ground with just enough industrial haze blowing over it to make it ideal for the job," wrote Gibson afterwards. *"The water was always calm because there was no wind in that valley."* The airmen needed a clear unimpeded view of the surface of the dam so that they could accurately determine their height by shining spotlights on the water. It was hair-raising flying, full of danger but Gibson had confidence in the men he had chosen.

Gibson turned his plane over the Derbyshire hills and lost height as he crossed Harden Moor and approached the tree-cloaked banks of Howden Reservoir. A few twists on the controls brought him into the narrow defile in which Derwent

Reservoir lay. He flew low over the water, passed the twin stone towers that marked the dam wall and made a climbing turn over the Snake Pass road to repeat the manouevre.

It may have been Gibson's plane that was seen by Land Girl Marjorie Walker who was peeling pit props in the woods above Ashopton. *"I was practically level with the aircraft,"* she said. *"It flew so low that we girls talked about it for many days afterwards."*

G for George dived over the lake several times but dusk, with mist, was beginning to fill the valley and visibility was down to a mile. Gibson tried once more. By this time the Australian bomb-aimer Pilot Officer Spam Spafford, perched in the nose of the plane, could hardly see the surrounding hills. There was a brief close-up of the water. Flight Lieutenant Trevor-Roper, in the rear gunner's turret, saw ripples on the water caused by the plane's slipstream and as Gibson climbed clear Spafford said over the intercom: *"That was bloody dangerous!"* Gibson admitted afterwards: *"Yes, we nearly hit the black water."* It had been a close shave.

Forty five years after the famous Dambusters' Raid a lone Lancaster bomber flies over the dam wall of Derwent Reservoir in 1988. Thousands of people lined the banks in tribute to the 50 airmen killed on the raid

Nevertheless, Derwent Reservoir was thought to be ideal for further practice flights. Early in May six Lancasters of the squadron flew low over the dam to test new bombsights, using angles on the towers to check their position. It was these planes that the Booths saw from their lonely home.

Nineteen Lancasters took off from Scampton on the night of May 16th. They destroyed the Möhne Dam, sending 134 million gallons of water flooding over the Ruhr, and breached the Eder Dam with similar effect. But eight planes failed to return and 50 airmen were killed. Gibson survived and was awarded the Victoria Cross. There were 32 other decorations for his comrades.

The villagers of the Derwent Valley could take pride in the fact that the great reservoirs near their homes had played a key part in one of the war's greatest feats of valour.

It was not only the RAF that took an interest in the Upper Derwent area. Troops moved into the valley early in the war. Anti-aircraft guns were sited on the towers of the Derwent and Howden Dams and their bases surrounded by tangles of barbed wire. Diamond shaped booms were moored on the water to make any seaplane landings by invading troops a considerable hazard.

After the successful Ruhr dams raid by the RAF, however, similar retaliatory raids by German bombers were feared. All the dams in the Pennines were thought to be at risk. In addition to the Derwent Valley reservoirs there were other stretches of water close by, including Strines, Langsett, Underbank and Midhope.

The 57th Anti-Aircraft Brigade, commanded by Brigadier B. Chichester-Clark, took over the South Pennines area. Five thousand troops were bivouacked by the sides of the reservoirs and searchlights and high-angled guns installed. Thousands of smoke cannisters were placed around the dams, some high on the hillsides, and they were connected by many miles of electric cabling so that in the event of enemy bombers approaching all could be activated at the press of a button.

At Strines and Midhope Reservoirs even more extensive measures to deter low-flying enemy planes were put in place. Giant lattice-work steel towers 300 feet high were erected by the Royal Engineers and steel hawsers strung across the water, each one carrying vertical cables weighted with concrete 30 feet above the surface. Any low-flying Heinkel or Dornier bomber trying to drop a bomb on the dam walls would have hit this spider's web of defences long before any damage could have been caused. Luckily for the Germans such an attack was never attempted.

The high moorland of the northern Peak District proved ideal for the training of tank crews and the remote area between the Upper Derwent Valley and the Little Don was soon littered with concrete blockhouses and mobile generators as more and more troops moved in. Tanks ploughed through the heather and many shells were fired at targets on Broomhead and Howden Moors. Needless to say, walkers were strictly prohibited.

While all this military activity was taking place life for civilians living in the Derwent Valley had to be carried on as usual. But times were changing and the villagers of Derwent and Ashopton had to face major upheavals in their lives due to the Ladybower Reservoir which was about to swallow their homes.

Work on the giant reservoir, to supply the water needs of Derby, Leicester, Sheffield and Nottingham, had started in 1935 and despite shortages of manpower and materials continued throughout the war. An immense 250-ft trench across the valley just north of Bamford was filled with 100,000 tons of concrete, then masses

The village of Ashopton was demolished when the Derwent Valley was flooded in 1945 to form Ladybower Reservoir. German and Italian prisoners of war were recruited to help build this immense concrete viaduct which now carries the A57 road from Glossop to Sheffield over the sunken village

of stone piled on either side of a 30-ft wide clay core to create the dam wall.

When the war started more than 300 men were working on the site but so many left on necessary wartime duties that only 200 were there six months later. German and Italian prisoners of war were brought to the site by coach from their camps at Burbage and Sudbury to supplement the work force at the dam and in Ladybower Quarry just off the Moscar road.

In July 1941 the evacuated girls of Notre Dame School abandoned the dark-beamed and wainscotted rooms of Derwent Hall to return to Sheffield, and the handsome building which was built in 1672 was dismantled. The last service was held in Derwent Church on March 17th 1943 and the sluice gates in the dam wall were closed the following day. The water began to rise and was soon lapping the foundations of the demolished Ashopton Inn and the piers of a new viaduct built to carry the Glossop to Sheffield road across the valley.

On September 25th 1945 the new reservoir was opened by King George VI and Queen Elizabeth who were making their first official visit to Derbyshire.

Many of the workers at the Avro plant at Woodford in Cheshire, where Lancaster bombers were assembled and test-flown before being handed over to the RAF, were recruited in the nearby Peak District

But the part that the Derwent Valley had performed during the war was commemorated in 1954 by a notable film *The Dam Busters*. Richard Todd, who played the part of Guy Gibson, was on board a Lancaster bomber that flew over the Derwent Reservoir in 1988 and when the flight was repeated in 1993, on the 50th anniversary of the Ruhr darns raid, thousands of people gathered on either side of the gaunt stone towers to see Britain's remaining veteran Lancaster bomber roar low over the water.

This dramatic spectacle awakened many memories. Basil Feneron, who was a flight engineer on one of the planes in 1943, said: *"There were tears in my eyes. It brought it all back again."* He was not the only one to experience similar emotions.

Ladybower Reservoir today, from Whinstone Lee Tor looking towards the tree-cloaked slopes of Hagg Side. The Derwent Dam lies just around the corner

The usual wear for girls who joined the Women's Land Army was a V-necked jumper and a pair of khaki knee-breeches. This was a typical poster that helped to recruit 80,000 women by June 1944. Their duties in the Peak District ranged from milking cows to killing rats

Chapter Eight
Girls on the Land

Many Peak District farmers depended on horses during the Second World War - it was only after 1945 that tractors began to replace them in large numbers.

All the heavy work on the farms was performed by horses. They pulled two-wheeled milk floats around the villages, hauled mowing machines, hay tedders and chain harrows across the fields and in high sunmer brought towering loads of hay back to the barns in four-wheeled carts.

In the hot summer of 1940 Dakins Farm in Chinley echoed to the abrasive sound of scythes being sharpened and the excited barking of several collie dogs. An iron-wheeled mowing machine, its long set of glistening teeth freshly oiled, was pulled out of the stone barn by farmer Harold Longden and harnessed to his horses Polly and Queenie either side of the centre shaft.

Dakins Farm at Chinley. In the large hay barn next to the farm house Pat O'Brien slept on a blanket amid the cobwebs. Two horses did all the heavy work during the war. It was not until 1946 that farm owner Harold Longden bought his first tractor

When the long grass in the big Hallgate Meadow had been left to dry and was gathered by Mr Longden and his clutch of perspiring helpers - all wearing braces over their open-necked shirts and handkerchiefs knotted around their heads - the horses pulled a cart piled high with hay back to the roadside farm.

Elsie Longden, the farmer's wife, and milk maid Pattie Clark, a rosy-cheeked girl of 19, waited in the yard with bottles of lemon barley water and thick ham rolls as the setting sun cast long shadows over the shippons, stables and hen coops. In the farm kitchen stood a polished Yorkshire range. Rashers of home-cured bacon hung from an iron hook, dripping fat on to warm oatcakes stacked on plates below.

Amid the tired group of haymakers was Pat O'Brien, a jovial red-faced Irishman who turned up at Dakins Farm each summer. He was said never to have stopped walking since he got off the boat at Liverpool. He slept on a blanket amid the hay and cobwebs in the main barn and kept a well-worn suit in a cardboard case at his side.

But 1940 was the last summer Pat was seen at the farm. He volunteered for the British Army and, some said, was later killed in Burma. Milk maid Pattie also left the farm that winter. She joined the WAAF and never returned to a farming life.

Pat, in fact, was not the only itinerant farm worker to sleep in a barn. Ron Hall, who was employed at Coldeaton Farm near Alsop-en-le-Dale in 1940, remembered a man called Jim who slept in a corner of the loft on a bed of hay. *"He came into the farm house for his meals,"* said Ron. *"That was how he liked it."*

There were eight shire horses, 70 milk cows, 150 sheep, four young Shorthorn bulls and an excellent sheepdog called Fellow at Coldeaton. Several large fields overlooking the gorge of Wolfscote Dale were ploughed to grow potatoes, turnips, kale, oats and wheat.

Migrant workers from Ireland arrived at Roystone Grange Farm near Parwich in late June to help with the hay-making for a month. They were paid £2 a week and slept in the barn before moving on to Cambridgeshire for the pea and potato harvest. This farm had ten working horses, two of them stallions that were in great demand for servicing mares across the Peak. Farmer John Etches and four other men cared for about 30 dairy cows milked by hand beside the farmyard pond, 70 beef cattle and a dozen pigs. But oats, turnips and potatoes were grown in the fields as well as 100 acres of grass for winter food.

Peak District farmers were encouraged by War Agricultural Executive Committees to expand food production in view of the threat to imported foods by German U-boats. The local area "War Ags" checked on farmers' performances, offered advice and allocated scarce resources such as animal feed and fertilisers. They also had far-reaching powers to evict farmers who refused to comply.

But not all the land was suitable for conversion from cattle or sheep grazing to the growing of crops. Donald Morten, who farmed at Cowdale, near Buxton, had particular difficulty. *"The ground was just not suitable,"* he said. *"Our potatoes were terrible, all shiny and hard. We grew as few as we could get away with. Turnips and mangolds were not too bad and we managed to grow some large cabbages. But the bad weather did not help."*

The Elliotts who farmed at Hope found the ground more suitable than Cowdale. In fact, potato picking on their farm became a useful money spinner for local people.

On bleak Rushup Moor, between Chapel-en-le-Frith and Castleton, Alan Virtue ploughed 20 acres to cultivate kale, swedes and potatoes in rotation. *"The Red King spuds grew well,"* he said. *"But the swedes were only moderate."* Jim Chadwick of Back Lane Farm, near Onecote, kept 40 cattle on 70 acres of "roughish" ground. The war brought feeding problems for his stock and he was glad when he was able to turn out the cattle to graze in May each year.

In February 1940 "summer time" was introduced early and retained all year round until 1941 when it was replaced for the summer months by "double summer time". Although this assisted many people returning home from work in the blackout it was a mixed blessing for farmers. *"It was dreadful,"* said Donald Morten. *"We started work at 6am, winter and summer, so that when the clocks were moved two hours forward in summer it meant we were actually starting at 4 am. Nights were light and labour scarce so we were having to manage on four or five hours' sleep at night."*

Many farmers had to manage by themselves. Ronald Thorp at Gorse Bank Farm, Baslow, for example, ploughed his fields each day during the war from 7am to 10pm. *"He was sometimes working by moonlight,"* said his wife Jessie.

In the harsh winter of 1939-40 Britain's farmers received a subsidy of £2 for every acre of grassland they ploughed. By the end of 1941 nearly 2,000,000 more acres of permanent grassland had been uprooted by the plough. Livestock farmers protested but the Ministry of Food insisted that an acre of crops fed many more people than an acre of grass.

As the war progressed and the U-boat menace began to recede the Government eased the pressure on sheep and cattle farmers. Hill sheep farmers, in particular, received large subsidies and some became quite prosperous.

One of the biggest problems for farmers, however, was labour. Although some farmers and their sons were able to avoid conscription by proving that the economic efficiency of their farm would otherwise be harmed, only men over 60 years of age and those who were declared physically unfit for military service could be sure of retaining their employment on the land.

By March 1940 Britain's agricultural industry had lost more than 30,000 men to the Armed Forces and nearly 20,000 to other more financially attractive occupations. Unskilled labourers constructing camps and factories for the army and the munitions industry were drawing double the pay of farm workers, for example.

Part of the solution was the formation of the Women's Land Army. Many of these girls lived in hostels, but most worked for individual farmers and lived with the family.

Schoolchildren helped to dig for vegetables and stack corn on Peak District farms. This girl, evacuated from Southend, clears cabbages on Rushup Edge near Chapel-en-le-Frith

The girls, who came from all walks of life, wore distinctive clothing. One 17 year-old volunteer who was directed to a Peak District farm was excited when her uniform arrived. She said: "It consisted of a dark beige knee-length overcoat, a slouch felt hat with badge, working shirts, two woollen V-necked jumpers, two pairs of khaki knee-breeches, three pairs of knee-high wool socks, dungarees, cotton twill overalls, a pair of wellingtons, leather ankle boots, steel heel-capped shoes, a green tie and a green armband with a red crown embroidered on it."

The girls' work varied. Rispah Bradshaw, who came from Sheffield, delivered milk to housewives around Buxton. Another girl was sent to a farm in Macclesfield Forest, three miles from the remote Cat and Fiddle Inn. *"I worked with the farmer to run his 80-acre farm,"* she recalled. *"We milked 40 cows by hand twice a day and cured our own bacon and ham."*

Other girls remembered cutting down hay ricks - *"tucking our dungarees into our socks and killing mice with pitchforks"* - and some girls had to work as rat-catchers. One Land Girl sent to a Peakland farm ran for her life when a rat hunt started but other girls were less squeamish. In fact, two young Land Girls in Lincolnshire even caught 12,000 rats in one year!

Other duties in the Peak included potato planting, cleaning pigsties and spraying fruit trees. Many girls were in the WLA's "Timber Corps", felling trees, stripping bark, working in sawmills and selecting trees for poles or general timber. Some 6,000 were in this corps. On the Chatsworth Estate 500 acres of immature 30 to 40-year-old coniferous trees were cut down to provide 1,000,000 cubic feet of timber for wartime needs. Ralph Gregory of Darley Dale and other timber

Land girls working for the Timber Corps

merchants paid the Duke of Devonshire £50 an acre for the wood, most of which was used for pit props.

Land Girl Marjorie Walker of Bamford worked for the "Timber Corps" in the Derwent Valley. *"We peeled pit props and sawed railway sleepers for the coal mines,"* she said. *"Heavier wood was also sawn and rolled down the hillside to a saw mill just above Ashopton."*

About 1,000 young women volunteered for the Land Army at the outbreak of war and by June 1944 there were 80,000 of them working on the land. Nevertheless, the farmers still needed more help. Alan Virtue was assisted by the evacuated girls of Westcliff High School when it was harvest time at Rushop House Farm. *"They soon learned how to make the corn sheaves into stacks,"* he said. *"Six girls came along with a teacher. I collected them by car and took them back. They also got a good farmhouse meal at the end of the day."*

By law school children had to be volunteers and at least ten years old. They were allowed to work a maximum of 24 half days a year and were paid sixpence an hour. David Turner and Graham Elliot, both then aged 12, were swift to volunteer and they worked on several farms around the village of Eyam. Their jobs included hoeing turnips (*"a hard and boring job,"* said David), clearing thistles and picking potatoes.

Another source of labour was the increasing number of prisoners of war, many of whom were camped in the Peak District. By July 1943 40,000 Italians were

German prisoners of war were often seen on Peak District farms. They wore a distinctive chocolate-coloured uniform

working in the fields of Britain, some billeted with farmers, and they were soon joined by German PoWs.

The Elliotts welcomed a Lithuanian named Luke to their farm at Hope. He lived in a shed in the yard but went into the farm kitchen for his meals. Another PoW who worked on the Caudwells' farm at Rowsley showed his gratitude by carving a jewellery box from a piece of wood and presenting it to Mrs Minnie Caudwell *"for her kindness"*. Two PoWs worked for Donald Morten at Cowdale - one of them, a former engineer from Hamburg, made children's toys in the evenings when farm work was over..

Life on the farm did have its compensations, of course. *"There was plenty of food about,"* said Jim Chadwick. At Onecote a local policeman was often called upon, quite unofficially, to kill a pig. *"We could kill two pigs if we wanted to,"* said Mr Chadwick. *"We used to salt the bacon and hang it in my bedroom inside a pillowcase, and we always saved ham for the harvest."*

The Elliotts at Farfield Farm in Hope fattened a pig through the summer and killed it in the autumn. Eva Elliott salted the flesh to make bacon, cured the ham, made black pudding from the blood and brawn from the head. She rendered down the animal's fat to make lard for cooking and to create most delicious crackling. There were no freezers in the farm kitchens of those days so neighbours shared the meat around. Rabbits could also be a useful source of income - young Charles Etches of Roystone Grange Farm once caught 58 in one evening - and Sheffield butchers were always eager to buy them.

Six years of war led to the modernisation of Britain's farms - something which some experts said might have taken decades in peacetime. The introduction of large numbers of tractors, despite the competing demands for the construction of military vehicles, made all the difference. In 1939 there were 56,000 tractors in use in Britain. By 1946 there were 203,000, though horses were still far more numerous.

It was 1948 before Ralph Twigge introduced his first tractor at Roystone Grange, and farmer Harold Longden bought his first tractor at the same time. Soon afterwards trailers, seed-spreaders, disc harrows, multi-blade ploughs and a wide variety of other mechanical devices began to fill his cobbled farmyard at Chinley. The horses Polly and Queenie, now rather elderly, went off to the knacker's yard and their stable was converted into a vehicle store. Farming in the Peak would never be the same again.

At Smedley's Hydro, the most impressive building in Matlock and now used as the
Derbyshire County Council offices, British officers were trained in intelligence techniques.
"The place is too crowded" complained author Evelyn Waugh, serving in the Royal Marines

Close to Smedley's Hydro was Rockside Hydro which was used as a psychiatric hospital for
non-commissioned officers in the RAF. By 1942 there were 849 patients at the hydro.
The building is now deserted, many of its windows broken

Chapter Nine
Troops at the Hydro

Quarrymen cycling to work along the old Roman highway of Batham Gate in 1941 were often startled by explosions that echoed around the cliff faces of a disused quarry at the side of the narrow road. Barbed wire surrounded the old limestone workings in Wainwright's Quarry at Peak Dale and an armed sentry stood at the entrance near the village Co-op. *"We were testing explosives in very primitive conditions,"* said former soldier Harry Berrisford.

The Peak District is situated in the heart of England and was far from any active war front. Limestone quarries which had been worked out and were now vast craters in the countryside, were ideal places to carry out ammunition experiments with minimal risk to the civilian population.

Imperial Chemical Industries manufactured bombs and shells in their plants at Glasgow and Birmingham and sent them to Peak Dale. The Ministry of Defence was particularly keen to check the effectiveness of lightweight bombs developed for the Blacker Bombard, intended for Home Guard use, the Piat mortar and the Jeffrey's Shoulder Gun. All were to be tested for their ability to penetrate armour-plating on German tanks.

"We fired thousands of rounds at targets placed on the side of a high cliff," said Harry Berrisford. *"Many unexploded bombs fell into a flooded part of the quarry and it was a ticklish job to retrieve them."*

Harry, a former ICI employee who had been discharged from the army on medical grounds, was one of the gunners at the site. Their only protection was a low concrete blast wall on the quarry floor. Inevitably, there were occasional accidents. A premature explosion as a mortar was fired from the Piat barrel ripped off several of Harry's fingers and only swift first-aid action by a colleague saved his life.

"I was back on duty after eleven weeks," said Harry. *"Then there was a second accident. Another premature explosion sprayed me and three other men with fragments of shrapnel. I was hit in the leg, wrist, back and buttocks but, amazingly, the other chaps escaped injury."*

Private Harry Berrisford was recruited to test explosives in a quarry at Peak Dale. "Many unexploded bombs that we fired fell into a pool and it was a ticklish job to retrieve them," he said. Harry was twice injured by premature explosions

The army established camps and bases in several parts of the Peak, perhaps the most secret and noteworthy being their requisition of Smedley's Hydro overlooking the town of Matlock. In this bleak, castellated, blacked-out Victorian building many British officers were trained in intelligence techniques. Patrick Leigh Fermor, the author and traveller, recalled a ball that young officers organised in the autumn of 1941. There were balloons, streamers and a small band. Henry Howard, one of the instructors, invited a young couple from nearby Chatsworth House. They danced together most of the evening. The man, a tall, slim ensign in the Coldstream Guards, and the girl, the youngest Mitford sister, were married soon afterwards. They were to become the future Duke and Duchess of Devonshire.

Evelyn Waugh, the famous author of Brideshead Revisited who was then a captain in the Royal Marines, was posted to Smedley's Hydro in May 1942 for a five-week course on photographic interpretation. He found the centre a very easy-going military establishment. The vice-commandant was Stanley Casson, a 53 year old Oxford don.

"Messing is very poor and the place too crowded," commented Waugh in his diary but he was intrigued by Matlock Bath and its *"petrified bowler hats"*. Waugh's wife joined him during the course and they stayed *"illicitly"* at the New Bath Hotel, visiting Chatsworth with Lady Anne Hunloke, sister of the 10th Duke of Devonshire, and touring the Derbyshire countryside.

Close to the Intelligence Training Centre stood Rockside Hydro which the RAF had taken over in 1940. This was a hospital for victims of stress or combat fatigue.

One young wife accompanied her husband, a flight sergeant who had been wounded during a bomber raid on Luxembourg, from London to Matlock in September 1940. *"He was being sent there for recuperation,"* she said. *"We arrived with two suitcases and took a taxi to Rockside Hydro. The staff there were a little surprised to see me but they helped me find accommodation in the town."* The couple met most afternoons, went to the Palace Cinema and walked up to Riber Castle.

By 1942 there were 849 patients - all NCOs - in the Hydro. Many were suffering from severe nervous exhaustion. The unfortunate expression "lack of moral fibre" became widespread and local pubs were ordered not to serve drinks to the men who wore a special uniform - a blue jacket, red tie and white shirt. Rockside Hydro, though staffed and administered with tact and understanding, was a rather unhappy place in the quiet peace of Derbyshire. About 80 RAF and WAAF personnel, many of them medical orderlies, staffed Rockside. They were billeted in Oldham House, next door to the hydro. In command was Group Captain Sir John McIntyre.

The hilly nature of the Peak District deterred the Air Ministry from siting any

Troops marching in Smedley Street. Matlock

airfields north of Ashbourne but the flatter countryside in the south of Derbyshire was thought to be suitable for flying training. Contractors' vehicles moved into the Ashbourne area in 1941, demolished a farm and several private houses on Derby Road just a mile from the town centre and constructed a standard bomber airfield with three runways, one of them a mile long. Hangars for Wellington bombers and accommodation blocks for airmen were also erected.

The first aircraft flew in on July 10th 1942. At first No. 81 Operational Training Unit concentrated on advanced practice flights for pilots and navigators before they were posted to operational squadrons, then No. 42 OTU moved in with Whitley bombers and Blenheims. Four miles away alongside the Sudbury road a satellite airfield was constructed on Darley Moor in 1943. A squadron of Ansons and Oxfords was based here to train air gunners and wireless operators. The streets of Ashbourne were now filled with men and women in air force blue uniforms, the George and Dragon in the Market Place proving to be a popular hostelry for both airmen and WAAFs. Many years later an Ashbourne resident, then a boy,

The George and Dragon in the Market Place at Ashbourne - a popular inn for airmen and WAAFs stationed at the nearby RAF airfields

Troops of the 8th Training Battalion were billeted in the ornate Whitworth Institute at Darley Dale from October 1940. The building, now the Whitworth Hotel, had been given to the village by the Victorian industrialist and inventor Sir Joseph Whitworth who died in 1887

remembered seeing *"groups of airmen singing arm-in-arm as they walked along Dig Street after missing the last truck back to camp."* Why, one wonders, was this young lad out so late!

The RAF also established a base at Harpur Hill near Buxton, taking over Burlow Farm on the site of the present-day High Peak College and utilising a maze of tunnels in remote country half a mile away to store bombs. The work of No. 28 Maintenance Unit grew as the war progressed. More and bigger bombs arrived and had to be safely stored before being distributed to Bomber Command airfields across the country. When the tunnels were full these lethal weapons were stacked alongside lanes on Staker Hill and Upper Edge. Mary Wheeldon, a nine-year-old at the time, remembered seeing hundreds of bombs neatly stacked in the fields not far from her home in Pomeroy.

At one time an RAF unit was stationed in Lyme Park near Disley. They took over the workshop yard (where the present-day coffee shop is situated) and supervised the arrival of many military vehicles that were driven up from Bristol in 1941. *"The mess room in the workshop was the night duty office,"* recalled Hubert Rutter who was employed at Lyme as a plumber. The peaceful grounds were disturbed by Red Cross vans, de-icing vehicles and RAF lorries parked amid the protective trees of Crow Wood, and other vehicles filling the flat area below the Cage.

Colonel Gerry Underwood

Leslie Wright was in the Territorial Army training to be an army signaller when war was declared. He moved to Bakewell and later went to France, being rescued in May 1940 by the Royal Navy from a wrecked pier at Calais wearing only a few rags of uniform. He later became a Colonel

Military units were sited without warning in various parts of the Peak. Anti-aircraft guns were placed on the castellated stone towers of the Derwent and Howden Dams, searchlights and more guns were sited in Asker Lane, Matlock, and there were more searchlights at Cowburn near Edale, in Coplow Dale near Little Hucklow, on high ground at Stanton in Peak and on Blackshaw Moor near Leek. Troops of the 8th Training Battalion arrived in the Matlock area in October 1940. Many soldiers were billeted in the Whitworth Institute at Darley Dale, others in Wirksworth Town Hall, a florist's shop being converted into a guardroom and a telephone switchboard installed in the Red Lion Hotel.

An advance party of the 2nd (North Midlands) Corps Signals, under the command of Colonel Gerry Underwood, arrived in Bakewell in September 1939 and set up camp at Burton Closes and Haddon House on the Rowsley road. *"We had no mattresses, no crockery except a bowl each and we had to sleep on the hard wooden floors,"* said Leslie Wright. An officers' mess was created at the Rutland Arms Hotel and men were billeted throughout the town.

A serious influenza outbreak led to the Cooperative Hall in King Street being converted into an army hospital with thermometers showing 40 degrees of frost. Bakewell extended an enthusiastic welcome to the soldiers, the Society of Friends turning their meeting house into an excellent canteen. When the Signals left Bakewell their place was taken by the Royal Army Service Corps.

Some civilian organisations moved into the Peak from blitz-threatened cities. Part of the Palace Hotel in Buxton was taken over by the Civil Service, staff moving from London in the first months of the war, a corset factory at Ashbourne was commandeered by Rolls-Royce from Derby and aero engine parts manufactured there, the Firth-Derihorn company transferred armaments production from Sheffield to a "shadow factory" in Darley Dale, and Bernard Wardle's silk and cloth printing business moved into Whitehall Works at Chinley when their Bridgnorth premises were taken over by the Air Ministry in 1939. Thomas Singleton, a maker of pearl buttons and handles, moved from Sheffield into the old Victoria Mill at Hathersage and turned out parts for aircraft - and buttons for military uniforms!

Camouflage nets were made by eight young women at William Edwards and Sons' factory in the village of Charlesworth. They received high wages, working 12 hours a day six days a week. The factory also produced steel helmet lacings and lanyards for rifles. This plant was typical of many small firms making small but important components for military use.

The DP Battery works at Lumford Mill in Bakewell manufactured batteries for the Royal Navy's submarines, lead and acid arriving at the town station in special wagons and being transported to the mill by lorry. The heavy batteries were also despatched by rail from Bakewell direct to the ports.

One particularly unusual activity was carried on at Brookfield Hall, a large Victorian house in ten acres of remote woodland which stands 1,400 feet above sea level on the Buxton to Whaley Bridge road. High-ranking naval officers and engineers based here worked on secret designs for submarine warfare, one device perfected being a special hatch mechanism to enable crews to escape from submerged craft.

High above Castleton, the famous Blue John Mine. Vital supplies of radium for the treatment of cancer were stored here deep below ground

Tourists who flock into the Peak District today and explore the deep water-worn caverns of the Blue John Mine at Castleton are perhaps unaware of the advanced scientific laboratory established there during the war years.

In 1939 the Christie Hospital in Manchester possessed more radium for the treatment of cancer than all Europe put together and it was decided to store it safe from air attack in the Blue John Mine. Even during the Manchester blitz in 1940 patients from many parts of Britain received treatment without interruption, among them a French legionnaire and even a Luftwaffe pilot.

The scientists who worked below ground were kept warm with hot coffee, their light provided by a generator at the top of the cavern. Supplies of radon gas, which was discharged from pure radium salt, were driven to Manchester each day, although it sometimes meant digging through snowdrifts to reach their car parked below Mam Tor. Later in the War, when the risk of air raids receded, the vital radium was returned to Christie's and placed down a 40-foot borehole in the hospital grounds.

Petrol storage dumps were established in country areas across Britain. One was sited in Dove Holes behind a high steel fence and guarded by troops. Lines of railway tank wagons were frequently shunted into the enclosure and petrol pumped into three large grasscovered underground tanks. More tanks were sunk in the disused Heathcote Quarry off Dale Road, a pipeline linking them to the tanks near Dove Holes Station. Army sentries were billeted in the village's Co-op Hall.

Many of the country's petrol dumps were also linked together by a pipeline that ran from coast to coast so that ships discharging their vital cargoes of important fuel could berth on either the east or west coast without the distribution of the oil being disrupted.

An underground pipeline was laid from Dove Holes through Sparrowpit to link up with the main west-east pipeline below Rushup Edge. This ran from the Mersey Estuary through Cheshire, entering Derbyshire near New Mills and passing through the Hope Valley into Yorkshire. Its course was marked by concrete stiles at each fence or wall it crossed. *"I remember excavating machines, which were quite new to us, digging a trench through the marshy land near Peakshill Farm,"* said one schoolboy from Sparrowpit. *"Soon afterwards lengths of black steel pipe were brought up by lorry."*

Much of the pipeline is still in use, 60 years later, by the Ministry of Defence. This was highlighted in March 2000 when contractors working for British Gas accidentally severed the pipeline at Furness Vale and sent 8,000 litres of aviation fuel flooding over nearby roads.

It was not just British personnel who were housed in camps established throughout the Peak between 1939 and 1945. In the early battles of the desert war in Libya and Egypt thousands of Italian troops were captured by the British army and many of them were sent to this country. PoW camps were set up, and it was not long before captured German airmen and seamen were added to the throng. Italians were most frequently seen in guarded working parties in the Peak, and many of the soldiers stayed on after the war and made friends with local people.

About 45 Italian PoWs were housed in a camp near Biggin and were usefully employed at the Derbyshire Silica fire-bricks works at Friden. There was a large PoW camp at Sudbury, just south of the Peak District, and others near Chesterfield and Nottingham. Groups of prisoners accompanied by British armed soldiers travelled 30 or 40 miles to work each day on farms or quarries in the Peak or on the giant Ladybower Dam being constructed in the Derwent Valley.

Three lorries carrying Italians from Chesterfield to the quarries in Stoney Middleton frequently called at Elizabeth Hawley's tiny sweet shop at Over End in Baslow. They were seeking cigarettes, which were in short supply, and as the shop had room for only about four customers at a time patient prisoners would form a queue in the road outside.

As the war progressed a separate PoW camp was established between Calver and Stoney Middleton but when Italy surrendered to the Allies armed guards were removed from the camp gates. *"The Italians were able to move about in quite an unrestricted way,"* said David Turner of Eyam. *"This tended to get up the nose of the few young locals who were not old enough or fit enough to be in the forces."* The lads of Eyam, Stoney Middleton and Calver challenged the PoWs to a football match and the prisoners were soon practising behind the barbed-wire fences in plimsolls and sandals. On the day of the match the Italians humiliated the locals by winning 9-0.

Another camp - for German PoWs - was set up in Buxton on the site of the present-day Burbage Primary School. When he returned to Buxton in the 1990s former paratrooper Werner Butz, who had been captured in Normandy in 1944, recalled the many friends he made during the war years. He and his comrade Herbert Biendara were invited into the home of a Buxton family living in Green Lane at Christmas time. It was a gesture they never forgot.

Karl Lohkamp, who was captured in Holland in November 1944, was brought to a "PoW hostel" in the centre of Dove Holes village in 1945. *"About 40 of us worked at Taylor Frith's"*, he recalled. *"The first weeks were terrible and we had aching arms and legs."* Fraternisation with British people was forbidden but the Germans soon established close relations with the quarrymen. When the war ended about 200 PoWs were in the Dove Holes camp, sleeping in six wooden barracks.

The British army camp at Burton Closes in Bakewell was taken over for German PoWs when the European war ended in May 1945. The commandant, Lieutenant Colonel Victor Holland, later settled in the town and often spent his holidays in Germany with former PoWs he had befriended.

The United States entered the war at the end of 1941 and increasing numbers of GIs began to arrive in Britain during 1942. Nearly two million were eventually stationed in the country, most of them being billeted in the southern counties. The only major U.S. army camp set up in the Peak District was *"Fort Anzio"* on Blackshaw Moor near Leek. Ben Dziwuloki recalled: *"We came to the camp on the moor in May 1944 with a permanent staff of 12 officers and 59 men. We processed thousands of GIs through the camp, gave them guns and sent them on their way to Normandy."*

In the camp were mess halls and a recreation room for table tennis in which dances were held. *"Local girls were brought in by church organisations,"* said Ben. He also remembered enjoying cycle rides around the Roches.

The novelty of American soldiers in battle gear parading through the streets of Leek soon wore off. Nora Clarke commented: *"They marched up Mill Street in their rubber-soled boots and you could hear this woosh-woosh noise most days. They would throw down half-a-crown for a few pennyworth of chips and not bother to pick up the change. They also gave lots of candy and chewing gum to local children. They may not have been very smart but they were very polite."*

Geoff Fisher a teenager in the town at the time also remembers well the first sound of the GI's soft shoe, out of step marching into the town - the boys thought it was a steam engine coming! He also remembers their generosity. The senior officer came to give the boys a talk at the school and when he asked the head if there was

The Blackshaw Moor army camp pictured just after the War

anything the school was desperate for, he was told there had been no wood for woodwork classes for some while. The next day a lorry arrived loaded with ten very large and well made wooden crates, which the boys set to dismantling.

Ben Dziwuloki's wife Barbara was an English girl who lived with her parents at the Britannia Inn in West Street. She remembered the GIs on parade in the Drill Hall in Alma Street. *"A cafe known as 'Doughnut Dugout' was opened for U.S. soldiers only,"* she said. Barbara dated Ben and they were married in St Mary's Church, Leek, in September 1945.

Camp followers, however, were inevitably a problem on Blackshaw Moor. Typical of them were three women - one a British soldier's wife with a young child - who spent a night in the camp after an evening out with three GIs in May 1945. They were apprehended the following morning and appeared in court at Leek, each being fined a fiver.

Soon after the end of the War, the U.S. troops departed and the sounds of bugles blaring and the shouts of command were no longer heard. Once more the only sounds on lonely Blackshaw Moor were the calling of curlews, the cackle of grouse and the bleating of lambs.

60 years on - two volunteers play the parts of
an American GI and his girl at a War Weekend
at Rowsley station, 2001

Chapter Ten
Drill in the Car Park

It was inevitable that the exploits of Britain's armed forces in the Second World War, displayed vividly in daily newspapers and in every newsreel at the cinema, should appeal to young teenagers.

The first service department to take advantage of this enthusism was the Air Ministry which, in January 1941, mobilized eager boys aged between 16 and 18 into the Air Training Corps. The corps, which still exists and is enthusiastically supported, was Britain's first state-directed, regimented youth movement. Within six months of its launch more than 200,000 cadets had volunteered and been enrolled.

The corps was as popular in the towns and villages of the Peak District as everywhere else in Britain. In Buxton, for example, 70 lads turned up at the Gas Service Buildings on March 27th for an inaugural meeting of No. 1180 Squadron. Mr J.H. Coleburt, a flying officer in the First World War and now in a reserved occupation with the Inland Revenue, was nominated as commanding officer of the squadron and it was announced that about 100 cadets were required.

There was no shortage of volunteers, largely due to the provision of RAF-style uniforms for the boys, and flights attached to the Buxton squadron were swiftly established at Chapel-en-le-Frith and Whaley Bridge. Kents Bank School in Buxton, and later a large house in St John's Road, became the squadron headquarters.

The first cadet to be enrolled at Buxton was Arthur Brown. One of his fellow cadets said: *"All we had for uniform at first was an air force-style forage cap on which we pinned the ATC's silver metal badge. Later, however, tunics and trousers arrived and we began to feel like real airmen."*

The man invited to organise the formation of C Flight in Chapel-en-le-Frith was Mr E.J. Cook, a branch manager of the Trent Valley and High Peak Electricity Company, who was proud of his rank as a Royal Navy commander in the First World War. This stocky, enthusiastic and hard-working officer was instrumental in recruiting about 30 boys from Chapel and the surrounding district and arranging for an RAF corporal at the Harpur Hill base to drive to the Ferodo works car park (an area now covered by private houses) for drill practice each Wednesday evening.

Across from the King's Arms Hotel was the surgery of local doctor William Cogan and into his claustrophobic dispensary (one boy said he had never seen so many bottles of medicine stacked on shelves to the ceiling) the cadets were given medical inspections before being marched down Market Street to a local store to be weighed. Even marching in formation was a novel and exhilarating experience for these embryo pilots and air gunners of the future.

One evening of each week was reserved for aircraft recognition at Chapel School in High Street. Mr James Clare-Lees, a respected professional man who was now a member ot the local Royal Observer Corps, displayed models of planes and projected silhouettes of British and German aircraft on to a screen. Often within a few seconds the boys became adept at identifying the stark outlines of the planes, including the more difficult front and side views.

Eventual recruitment into the RAF often depended on a reasonable knowledge of mathematics. Members of the ATC who were thought to be deficient in elementary algebra and trigonometry were given special lessons at Chapel School, Mr George Hallam, headmaster of Whaley Bridge Primary School, and Miss Alice Hughes, head of maths at the evacuated Westcliff High School, teaching the boys one evening each week.

Boys as young as 15 were allowed to join the ATC as the war went on. Instruction in navigation, map-reading, practical wireless and petrol engine technology were included in the curriculum - all intended to assist candidates joining the RAF at the age of 17 or 18. And, in Buxton at least, recreational facilities were provided. When off duty the boys could play billiards, darts or table tennis and visit a canteen that offered cups of tea and sandwiches.

In a further bid to encourage recruiting the Air Ministry arranged for groups of ATC cadets to visit RAF stations and be taken up in bombers to gain flying experience. This scheme was successful, although three boys from C Flight of 1180 Squadron came to a tragic end one day in September 1943.

Cadets Peter Bond, Denis Fox and Edward Hall, all aged 17, were spending a week at Syerston, an RAF base near Nottingham, when they were invited to join a practice flight in a Lancaster bomber. The lads eagerly grasped the opportunity. They were given padded clothing and squeezed into the aircraft alongside the radio

The Lancaster bomber

operator. But something went wrong and the plane crashed close to the airfield. Everyone on board was killed.

The graves of three Air Training Corps cadets who were killed when on a practice flight with the RAF in September 1943. Cadets Peter Bond, Dennis Fox and Edward Hall, all aged 17, are buried in Chapel-en-le-Frith churchyard

Three other cadets from the Chapel flight saw the accident happen. Roy Hill, who lived in Chinley, said: *"The plane hit the ground in a plume of smoke. We just could not believe it. We were taken home immediately."* The boys' funeral took place at St Thomas Becket Church in Chapel and scores of villagers joined the tragic family mourners at the gravesides.

In December 1941 all boys and girls aged between 16 and 18 were required to be registered for some kind of service and were encouraged to join an organisation that would fit them for national service when their time came.

In a bid to encourage more girls to join the Woman's Auxiliary Air Force a "Women's Junior ATC" was launched, more than 100 young women attending an inaugural meeting of the New Mills unit in the Town Hall in January 1942.

Another organisation was the Girls' Training Corps, which offered help to young women preparing for possible service in the armed forces. The Buxton unit, which had links with the ATC, the Sea Cadets and the Scout and Guide movement, was organised by Mrs Margaret Finlow, head of science at Silverlands Girls' School.

Detachments of Sea Cadets were formed from 1943 but the numbers of personnel required for the Royal Navy were not as great as those needed for the RAF and the Army.

The Army Cadet Force was launched by the War Office in 1942 with the attraction that boys as young as 14 would be able to wear khaki uniform and be trained as soldiers. A company of the 1st Derbyshire Cadet Battalion (the Sherwood Foresters) was formed at New Mills School, pre-service training taking place after school hours and at weekends. Fifty boys immediately joined under the command of Captain Harry Youd, their popular mathematics master. Physical training teacher Mr Percy Mallett gave instruction in the handling of weapons and map-reading, and field craft was supervised by Lieutenant Frederick Prior, the art master, and Lieutenant William Hoult, the English master.

Sixth-form science scholar and prefect Cecil Kay of Hathersage was promoted to company sergeant major and he accompanied three officers and 25 cadets to Chatsworth Park in August 1943 for a week under canvas.

One boy said: *"We had an exercise around New Mills one Saturday morning and Lance Corporal Alan Bennett led several of us through the church grounds back to the school where we 'captured' the HQ staff in the Art Room. I am afraid that Mr Youd was not very pleased."*

The Army Cadet Force proved so popular, in fact, that some Air Training Corps cadets also joined and had the benefit of choosing from two uniforms when setting out to impress their girl friends,

Boys who joined the Army Cadets in Wirksworth were based in the town's grammar school. They formed F Company of the 3rd Derbyshire Cadet Battalion (the Sherwood Foresters) and their talented sharpshooters and athletes won several trophies for which many cadet units competed.

There is no doubt that the training in leadership and responsibility which the corps gave proved to be a valuable asset when the boys eventually joined the armed forces.

Chapter Eleven
Put out that Light!

In the windswept limestone village of Peak Dale stood a small, single-storey building with a corrugated iron roof that was known in 1939 as *"Mrs Burton's Shop"*. Inside it was often difficult to find the counter due to the mass of household articles offered for sale. There were mops and mouse-traps, cotton reels and ribbons, hammers and nails, tins of polish and paint, cycle clips and carpets, pet food and dusters, stepladders hanging from the roof, tiers of shelves heaped with packets of garden seed, boxes of bulbs, candles and matches and, particularly noticeable by its aroma, a large tank of domestic paraffin, a form of fuel much used in country districts at that time.

Marie Burton, who lived near her shop in Upper End, was a true entrepreneur. If a villager wanted something she did not stock she would make a note and within a few days put a girl assistant in charge of the shop and walk a mile over the fields to Peak Forest Station from where she would travel to Buxton or even to a Manchester warehouse to ensure her customer was not disappointed.

One of the first effects of the declaration of war in September 1939 was a flurry of official notices giving the public advice on "air raid precautions." All windows and doorways emitting light at night were to be blacked out to prevent eagle-eyed German aviators locating their targets. Inevitably, this meant a rush to the shops for blinds, curtains, black paint and anything else that could be used.

Mrs Burton swiftly realised that black cloth to cover windows would rapidly become dear or unobtainable. *"Keep an eye on the shop,"* she told her assistant on the day before war was declared. *"I'm off to Manchester."* At a city warehouse she seized every roll of black curtain material she could lay her hands on and had it despatched by rail to Peak Dale. *"I sold out within two weeks,"* she said. *"I think everyone in the village bought their blackout material at my shop."*

Many people lined their heavy curtains with black fabric. Some trimmed this with braid or embroidery, others made frameworks of laths to fit inside the window frames, then nailed black paper to them.

The blackout transformed conditions of life in the Peak District more thoroughly than anything else during the war. Preventing light escaping from windows was a chore that became more and more tedious. At Chatsworth House most of the windows were fitted with large wooden shutters which were closed by the evacuated teaching staff of Penrhos College at dusk each night. Senior girls were sent outside to inspect the building for any specks of light. *"It was an eerie task on very dark nights,"* said former pupil Nancie Park. *"We had only a blacked-out torch to find our way around the building."*

At Bradwell and Bamford, Home Guardsmen patrolled the pitch-black village streets looking for escaping lights. *"We had to warn several people,"* reported Sergeant Fletcher.

The official blackout imposed at sunset on September 3rd was strictly enforced for several months. There were no street lamps and only dim sidelights could be used on motor vehicles. But in the spring of 1940 the restrictions were slightly eased. Hand torches could be carried if dimmed with a double thickness of white tissue paper (this started a constant search for torch batteries) and louvred masks for headlights, advertised in Buxton for example at 10s 6d each and looking like miniature top hats, could be fitted to motor vehicles. Council workmen slapped white paint on the walls of bridges and the railways painted the edges of station platforms to help passengers alighting in the dark.

Accidents in the blackout were inevitable, despite the introduction of "summer time" in February 1940. In Chapel Milton in the shadow of a high railway viaduct several people walking home from church one Sunday night were struck by a couple of cyclists and sent flying, luckily without serious injury, and in Bakewell and Matlock there were increasing reports of pedestrians colliding with street lamp-posts in the dark.

Magistrates were kept busy with the number of prosecutions for "failure to obscure efficiently" lights in shops and public houses. Fines of around £2 were usually imposed for showing lights in the New Mills area. At Buxton court on December 14th 1940 a householder was fined £1 15s (with 2s 9d costs) after a policeman spotted a bonfire in the man's garden. The constable told the court: "Only ten minutes after we had extinguished the flames with buckets of water enemy planes were heard overhead."

Many older men who were not required for military duty joined the Air Raid Precautions movement, donning blue overalls and wearing steel helmets bearing the letters ARP. One of their roles was checking the emission of lights in their respective villages. The organisation was set up in 1938 and hundreds of thousands of wardens had been recruited by the time war broke out.

Wardens' posts were established in every Peak District village. Dr Mary Andrews, a well-known figure in the Hope Valley, was particularly active as an air raid warden. She gave instructions on first aid to the local Home Guard and delivered several lectures on gas warfare and how to escape its most lethal effects in the Memorial Hall at Bradwell .

Following the Munich crisis in 1938 the fear of poison gas cannisters being dropped by enemy aircraft became almost an obsession with the Government. Throughout the country 38,000,000 gas masks were issued to men, women and children - 8,500 of them being handed out to the population of New Mills, for example .

During the war scare in 1938 some 38,000,000 gas masks were issued

Hitler will send no warning –

so always carry your gas mask

ISSUED BY THE MINISTRY OF HOME SECURITY

The threat of an enemy poison gas attack fortunately did not materialise

One historian has described the rubber and metal mask as being *"a grotesque combination of pig-snout and death's head"*. Once a week there was gas mask drill at the schools. Air entered through a black metal tube almost the size of a cocoa tin and was expelled between the soft rubber sides of the mask and the cheeks, making awful blubbering noises that appealed to all children. One pupil who attended Lady Manners School at Bakewell recalled: *"I can remember that rubbery smell of the gas mask to this day. And the noise when we donned them in class was like that of a thousand honking geese."*

There was a transparent plastic shield to see through but this swiftly became clouded by condensation, despite the use of vaseline to keep it clear. Each mask was packed in a stout cardboard box and was hung by a cord around the neck. Everyone was expected to carry their masks with them at all times but this practice lapsed as the war went on, although Geoff Fisher of Leek, a schoolboy at Leek High throughout the war, says that they had to take their mask to school every day during the War - and were sent home to get it if they ever forgot.

Despite the constant threat of gas warfare being waged against civilians the biggest fear proved to be fire, particularly when it became standard practice for enemy bombers to rain incendiary bombs across the countryside. By June 1940 about 68,000 stirrup pumps had been distributed to local authorities. Air raid wardens, police and members of the Home Guard received most of them but private individuals could purchase them - if they were available - for £1 each.

The pump was a slim metal tube that resembled a bicycle pump and it was fitted with a large, stirrup-shaped handle. The tube was immersed in a bucket of water and an attached length of hose directed at a blaze. It was quite simple to operate.

" Would you mind paying attention, Mrs. Eglethorpe, please : I hope you don't think they enclose directions with the bomb . . ."

Many demonstrations on the use of stirrup pumps were given to groups of householders. Although essential training many people thought it a joke and this cartoon was typical

Notices from the Ministry of Information were pinned up throughout the Peak District with the following recommendation on what to do before going to bed: *"Turn off the gas at the main, leave some water in the bath, fill a bucket and leave it handy together with a bucket of sand or fine earth. If you have to leave your home suddenly keep a bag packed with necessities you may need and have your gas mask near you. Leave additional clothing with a friend as a further precaution, put a pair of outdoor shoes and a warm coat by your bed in case of sudden emergency."*

Householders were urged to form "neighbour groups" to protect their property. A typical meeting was held in a field off Lightwood Road, Buxton, in July 1940. About 50 local people were given a demonstration on the use of a stirrup pump in tackling a blazing incendiary bomb by Captain Tom Brindley, area ARP organiser.

So many business premises in the towns were being destroyed by fire bombs showering from enemy planes that in January 1941 the Government introduced compulsory firewatching and all employees, including women, had to put in at least 48 hours each month. Rotas in all British towns were drawn up for this very unpopular duty, the firewatchers patrolling shops and factories and occasionally snatching a little sleep on makeshift beds.

The air raid wardens of Chinley pose outside the Princes Hotel. Fourth from the left on the front row is Jack Atkinson, an army captain in the First World War, who created controversy by criticising war "shirkers" in 1942. ARP wardens in Chinley and other Peakland villages took their voluntary responsibilities very seriously

Members of the National Fire Service based at Wirksworth pose for a group photograph with one of their engines in November 1944. On the front row is the senior officer, Mr Gallimore

Trailer pumps were rushed to the scene of incendiary bomb fires behind a car. This pump was given to the village of Hathersage by Sheffield industrialist George Lawrence of Jaggers Lane (standing on the right). Regrettably, Mr Lawrence was killed during the Sheffield blitz in

Demonstrations by local fire brigades always attracted crowds. This display amid the buttercups took place off Park Road in Chapel-en-le-Frith

There was no compulsion in country areas but difficulties in recruiting firewatchers in some Peak District villages were highlighted by Captain Jack Atkinson, a senior ARP warden at Chinley, in April 1942. His appeal for men to offer their services whenever an alert was sounded had produced only one volunteer *"In the event of a serious raid the 36 local wardens would find it impossible to guard effectively the 800 houses scattered over the four square miles of this area,"* a parish meeting was told.

Captain Atkinson was furious that some people did not seem to realise that there was a war on. After the meeting he said: *"There are many people who have left cities in order to get away from the war. When they are not called upon by their city employers to do firewatching they avoid any kind of work of civil or national importance and they are content to let those*

A fire engine towing a trailer pump and a converted pre-war car - key units in the National Fire Service at Chapel-en-le-Frith. Seen in Hayfield Road 1941

Buxton sub-division of the National Fire Service distinguished themselves at Matlock August bank holiday, 1944, by winning the Stoddart Cup. Leading Fireman Wildgoose holds the cup

St John Ambulance nurses at Chapel-en-le-Frith. On far left is Billy Wilkins, far right Sam Waterhouse. Dr Neil Kennedy sits centre front

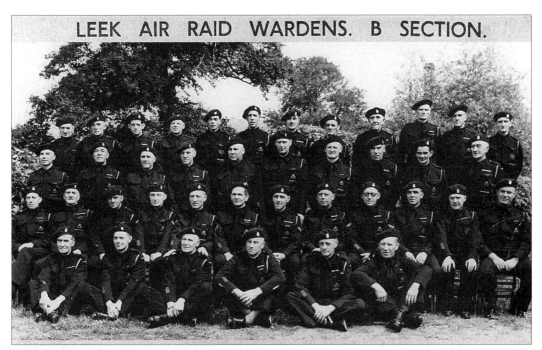

LEEK AIR RAID WARDENS. B SECTION.

H. Kirby H. Lovatt F. Goddard H. Clayton A. Pickford J. Watson W. Knott A. Hodgkinson C. Bowyer F. Fisher H. Knight E. Piercy
Centre :—P. Hamilton E. Hamnett P. Hall H. Potts G. Burnett A. Nadin H. Evans J. Bowcock J. Sales R. Large
Senior Senior Senior Senior Senior Senior
F. Tunnicliffe H. Harrison F. Maguire R. Hammerton F. Hulme W. Brookes L. Fisher F. Galton W. Nixon J. Turner H. Cope H. Prentice
Front :—J. Goodwin N. Williams M. Bestwick A. Jackson F. Hambleton E. Mathershaw

Above: Section of the Air Raid Wardens of Leek
Below left, two volunteers 60 years later wearing ARP uniforms during a War Weekend at
Darley Dale in 2001

Above, another group at Darley Dale just leaving
the railway station. The soldiers are 'home on
leave', and the woman is in typical forties' dress,
complete with basket and knitting wool

living in towns, and a few volunteers in the country, to do it for them."

A combined ARP exercise which called into action every local organisation in any way connected with air raid security and welfare was held at Chapel-en-le-Frith in February 1942. There were three incidents set up - at Whitestones, Horderns and Hill's Garage on Hayfield Road - where high explosive, incendiary bombs and liquid gas were assumed to have been used. Fire and rescue and contamination squads swung into action and conditions were made as nearly as possible those of a real air raid.

One of the rescue centres was the Constitutional Hall where "homeless" people were taken. There were 60 alleged casualties and a mobile canteen - very popular - was brought in. Umpires checked everyone's performance under the supervision of the ARP divisional controller Mr W.R. Sherwin.

Another big Civil Defence exercise covering all the High Peak occurred in July that year. Personnel taking part undertook their responsibilities very seriously and many lessons were learned.

During the Sheffield blitz more than 30 men and women trained in first aid were called out in Wirksworth and stayed all night at the village's ambulance post in case they were needed. They could see vivid white and yellow flashes of exploding bombs flickering across the crimson northern sky. As it happened, however, their services were not required.

In Leek the ARP established their headquarters in the Town Hall in Market Street and an ambulance bunker was set up in the Butter Market. In Dove Holes the village's wardens met in the Methodist Chapel.

Britain's numerous fire brigades were combined into a new National Fire Service in May 1941 and volunteers were enrolled into the Auxiliary Fire Service, most villages now having their own fire station, often in someone's garage, where grey-painted trailer pumps could be towed by lorries or private cars to the scenes of fires. *"I remember one becoming detached when we were speeding through Hathersage";* said a former AFS officer. *"Luckily no damage was done and, in any case, our call-out turned out to be a false alarm."*

Demonstrations were often mounted by the local firemen, the petrol-engined pumps using mill ponds to send streams of water arching into the sky, much to the delight of crowds who gathered to watch. Lakes such as the one in Buxton's Pavilion Gardens were used as emergency reserves for fire tenders that carried their own water supplies.

Any device that could be utilised to fight fires was brought out of storage. One of the oddest, perhaps, was a manual pump - looking little more than a wooden box on small iron wheels - that was put on standby to tackle any incendiaries that might fall on Chatsworth House. The pump had last been used in 1851 .

Chapter Twelve
Khaki and Blue

It was a jovial crowd of uniformed young men who climbed into a convoy of camouflaged lorries outside Buxton Drill Hall in July 1939. They were part-time soldiers of the Territorial Army looking forward to a month in camp on the East Coast and an intensive training course on anti-aircraft defence.

The peacetime strength of the TA had been rapidly expanded when Britain woke up to the threat of Nazi Germany after the Munich crisis of 1938. Little did the High Peak men realise that only a few weeks after returning home from camp they would be off again, this time in earnest when the outbreak of war meant immediate mobilisation .

Major Basil Darbyshire was in command of 370 men of the Sherwood Foresters. To their surprise they were again sent to the East Coast - to man "ack-ack" guns on the bleak Humber Estuary.

Young Harry Berrisford, who manned one of the unit's powerful searchlights, remembered meeting members of the crew of the Royal Navy light cruiser HMS Calcutta, then in Hull Docks for overhaul. The sailors challenged the soldiers to a darts match and Sapper Denis O'Grady of 359 Company - an enterprising soldier who was later promoted through the ranks to become commanding officer of the same battery - prepared an illustrated parchment scroll in acceptance. The High Peak men won the contest handsomely.

It was hoped that the mobile searchlights attached to the Humber battery would pick out high-flying enemy aircraft at night. *"Once we locked on to a plane we were assured that no matter how much the pilot twisted about our sensitive equipment would keep the plane in our beam,"* said Harry Berrisford. *"But we had few opportunities to test this theory at that period of the war."* The high-angle guns manned by the High Peak Territorials were quick-firing 3.7 inch weapons, the supply of which to the Army had been much accelerated after Munich.

In May 1939 the Government decided to double the size of the Territorial Army and in that month two companies, each of 175 men, were formed in Glossop. Each volunteer signed for a four-year engagement. While training he received 2s to 10s 9d a day according to his trade qualification and rank. Each year 15 days were to be spent at a training camp, with full pay and allowances for wives and families.

In July and August 1939 the Glossop men joined the 2nd (North Midland) Corps of Signals in camp at Skegness and when war was declared one line section was immediately sent to France. Later they were employed on the South Coast of England laying 880 miles of underground cable as part of the anti-invasion measures. As the war progressed they were posted to the Middle East and India in the 4th Corps of Signals.

Sergeant Brian Catlin of Chinley, right, at Koggala air base in Ceylon. He was shot down and captured by the Japanese in the Indian Ocean in 1942, and is seen above after his release from captivity in 1945

A Catalina flying boat similar to the aircraft in which Brian Catlin was shot down. The airman was badly burned and had 74 separate wounds. Three of his comrades were killed.

TA recruits in the east of the Peak joined the force in Chesterfield and, like the Glossop men, were in camp at Skegness when the war started.

The British Army soon began to be strengthened by an influx of volunteers and conscripts. Single men were the first to be registered for national service and by the end of 1939 1,500,000 men had been recruited. The age limit rose; at New Mills Employment Exchange in May 1941, for example, men up to the age of 39 were being registered - 127 of them. Ten expressed a preference for the Royal Navy, 42 for the RAF, six for Civil Defence and *"69 were left for the Army."* When manpower became even more acute the age limit was from 18 to 51 years of age.

Brian Catlin of Chinley was one of the eager lads who in 1936 forsook birdnesting in the fields around his home and volunteered for the Royal Air Force aged 16. By the time Japan entered the war he was a sergeant flight engineer serving with a Royal Canadian Air Force squadron at a remote base in the Shetlands. In April 1942 two Catalina flying boats from the base were sent out to the Indian Ocean and immediately ordered to mount patrols in search of a Japanese fleet reported to be heading towards Ceylon. Brian Catlin sat alongside his pilot, Squadron Leader Leonard Birchall, when a fellow member of the crew spotted several battleships and aircraft carriers 3,000 feet below. Catlin photographed the ships as Birchall ordered a sighting signal to be sent to Ceylon. Then Japanese Zero fighters turned up and cannon fire hit the Catalina.

The plane caught fire and crashed into the sea. All but one of the crew managed to scramble into the water, two more dying before the rest were picked up by the Japanese Navy. Catlin was badly burned. The surviving six airmen were beaten up and then taken to Japan for three years of barbarous captivity. But the Catalina's important radio message had been received in Colombo and annihilation of the British Eastern Fleet avoided. Catlin, incidentally, was later commissioned and finished his career in the RAF as a squadron leader.

Peak District men were in action throughout the war in various parts of the world. Again in the Indian Ocean Flight Sergeant "Ollie" Gomersal, who came from Buxton and worked in the Treasurer's Department at the Town Hall, found himself having a dramatic encounter with the enemy when he was the navigator of a Wellington bomber that sighted a U-boat off the Somali coast in May 1944.

The Wellington, piloted by Flying Officer Roy Mitchell, dropped depth charges and opened fire with tracer bullets. The U-boat was blown to the surface and then began firing back at the RAF plane. The battle raged for an hour. Mitchell's plane had to fly back to Scuiscuiban in Somalia to refuel but other aircraft resumed the attack. It took repeated attacks by five more Wellingtons before U-852 was eventually destroyed.

When Flight Lieutenant Bill Astell drove to Chinley Station one sunny morning in 1943 there were only two people with him in the family's black Austin car - his mother and his nine-year-old sister Heather. After all, he was just returning

Flight Lieutenant Bill Astell of Combs was killed on the Dambusters' Raid in 1943. He gained the Distinguished Flying Cross for "great courage and fortitude" when shot down in the Libyan desert the previous year

to his base after a normal seven-days' leave .

The 11.15 am train to Sheffield pulled out of the station on time and Bill, his peaked cap askew on his head, waved cheerily until his carriage vanished in drifting smoke. His mother and sister drove back to their home at Spire Hollins in Combs unaware that Bill knew he was about to take part in one of the most hazardous operations of the Second World War - the famous Dambusters' Raid .

Bill had been awarded the Distinguished Flying Cross earlier in the war for *"displaying great courage and fortitude"* after being shot down in Libya and surviving a five-day walk across the desert. He returned to Combs to recuperate, smoke his favourite pipe and sometimes go on rabbit hunts in the fields on Ladder Hill, his shotgun echoing around the hills that rim the Combs valley.

His wounds healed, he was eager to return to the war and, early in 1943, began to fly four-engined Lancaster bombers. Then he joined 617 Squadron at Scampton in Lincolnshire where the Dambusters' Raid was being prepared. When he reached Combs for a final leave in May 1943 he was quieter than usual and contented himself with long walks in the Peak District hills. He hinted to his sister Betty, who was in the WRNS, that *"something big"* was coming off but that was all.

Leaving home on the same day, and seen off from the same station by his 20-year-old fiancee, was another young airman, Sergeant Jack Marriott, who lived only two miles from Bill's home. He, too, was heading for the RAF bomber base at Scampton and would be in Bill Astell's flight on the night of May 16th.

Jack Marriott was also born in 1920. He lived with his parents, three elder brothers and a sister at Middleton House in New Smithy, a hamlet on the outskirts of Chinley, and attended the village school. For several years he was employed by J.J. Hadfield Ltd at their Forge bleachworks before joining the RAF and being trained as a flight engineer. By the time he joined 617 Squadron in 1943 he had flown on 27 bombing raids, including daring low-level daylight attacks on Le Creusot and Milan, and had been awarded the Distinguished Flying Medal.

On his last leave Jack attended Chinley Chapel and heard a sermon by the minister, the Rev. W. A. Powicke. Later he met his fiancee and she found him unusually subdued. He, too, said nothing about the forthcoming operation.

Although the dams' raid was a success eight of the 19 planes that took part failed to return. Bill Astell and his near-neighbour Jack Marriott were among those who died, Bill's plane exploding shortly after crossing the Dutch coast and Jack's Lancaster crashing after dropping its "bouncing bomb" on the parapet of the Eder Dam. Both men were buried in a British war cemetery in the Reichswald Forest.

More fortunate on the Dambusters' Raid was John Percival Nugent whose family lived in Stoney Middleton. John attended Hassop School and later became a teacher at a school in London. He joined the RAF, was trained as a navigator and was on board Flight Sergeant C. T. Anderson's plane, the last one to take off from Scampton.

A typical forces greetings card from Ismailia in Egypt. This airgraph was sent in 1943 by Aircraftman Harry White (later Mayor of High Peak) to his friend George Watson.

Another Peak District man, John Stanley Rowland of New House Farm near Chinley, volunteered for the RAF when war broke out and flew on 39 bombing raids. On one occasion the bombs on board his Halifax froze in their racks during a raid on the Italian city of Turin and Stan climbed down into the bomb bay to free them with a large spanner. On another raid the planes of his squadron destroyed V-2 rocket sites at Peenemunde.

Squadron Leader Colin Wilson, whose parents lived at Greyfriars in Combs, was awarded the DFC while serving with Bomber Command. Although slightly over-age for operational flights he, too, had volunteered for the RAF on the outbreak of war - he was an experienced pilot, having flown his own plane for several years in peacetime.

Another officer, Flight Lieutenant Billy Lingard of Bridgeholm, Chinley, flew

On their way to the Far East in May 1942 these servicemen from the Leek area posed for a group photograph on the troopship Dominion Monarch.
Standing (L to R) are A/c W.A. Patterson, A/c F. Ferns, A/c A.C. Whitehurst, P/te A. Grindey, P/O N.E. Bishop, L/Cpl J. Phillips, L/Ac H.P. Sherratt.
Sitting (L to R) are A/c F. Cooper, A/c J.C. Baker and A/c F. Torkington

in Coastal Command aircraft for three years before being sent to the United States to instruct British and American airmen in navigation techniques.

The death roll of servicemen from the Peak mounted as the war progressed. Nevertheless, the number of men killed was much lower than the appalling death totals of the First World War, and this can be seen today on war memorials throughout the country. One exception, however, is the village of Hathersage where 23 local men died in the 1914-18 war and as many as 22 in the 1939-45 war. *"This inequality is unusual,"* comments the Rev. M.F.H. Hulbert, a former vicar of Hathersage. In this particular case the explanation lies in the village's large growth in population between the two wars.

The father of David Bassett, who lived in Ilam, served in both the Boer War and the First World War, and it was particularly poignant when the villagers of Dovedale learned in 1944 that his youngest son had been killed. David, a flight engineer in the RAF, was shot down over Belgium. His two brothers were in the Army, one of them serving in his father's old battalion of the Grenadier Guards.

Another airman, Radio Officer Leonard Fred Mitchell of High Lea, New Mills, was proud to have been in the crew of a long-range aircraft flying Winston Churchill to the United States when the Prime Minister was meeting President Roosevelt. But Leonard died at sea in March 1943 and was buried in New Mills churchyard.

The first New Mills man to be decorated was Grenadier Guardsman George William Walton of Midland Terrace who won the Military Medal, but also his life, while serving as a Commando in the raid on St Nazaire in March 1942.

Another Military Medal was awarded to Sergeant John Carter of Leek for *"courage, leadership and devotion to duty"* in France in 1944. He volunteered for three fighting patrols while serving with the Royal Scots Fusiliers near Frenouville, stalking and killing at least three sentries with his Sten gun and hand grenades while *"mopping up"* enemy section posts. Unfortunately, 24-year-old Sergeant Carter was killed later in the year without hearing of his award.

The French honoured Sergeant Victor Clayton of Cornhill Street, Leek, with their highest award, the Croix de Guerre and Star in 1945, Victor's wife hearing the news from her husband just before V-E Day. The soldier had served with the signals section of a super heavy battery, Royal Artillery, in several battles in Italy, France and Germany.

Sergeant Richard Henry Tebbutt, who was well known as a butcher in Buxton after the war, served as a gunner in North Africa and Italy before landing at Arnhem with the 1st Airborne Division in 1944. He was one of the men who actually reached the famous bridge with Colonel John Frost's small force and was taken prisoner by the Germans.

Less fortunate were soldiers captured by the Japanese. Joseph Kenneth Farlam of Fairfield, Buxton, for example. He served with the Sherwood Foresters from 1939 and was a veteran of the Dunkirk evacuation. But he became a prisoner of war in the Far East and spent two and a half years working on the infamous Burma Railway and a further year in Japan before returning home.

During the retreat to Dunkirk, British troops defended the small French town of Oignies, 17 men from Buxton being killed there on one day in May 1940. It is little wonder that the Derbyshire town "twinned" itself with Oignies and established close links with its citizens in 1968.

The war's gruesome toll touched most villages in the Peak. Thirteen men from the Baslow area died, the vicar's son Basil Drew being one of the first.

Many servicemen witnessed events that are now part of Britain's history. Ray Walter of Buxton, serving on a landing craft just before D-Day, entered Southampton Water to find it crammed with ships ready to sail for Normandy. *"It was one of the most moving and emotional sights I have ever experienced,"* he said. One of the men who landed in Normandy on D-Day was Harold Merrick of Chinley who also remembered playing an improvised game of cricket on the beach at Dunkirk while waiting to be rescued in 1940.

Tom Gregory, who later became well-known as chauffeur to the Mayors of Buxton, waded ashore on to a Normandy beach on D-Day in June 1944 and celebrated his 21st birthday sheltering in a foxhole.

Gunner Cecil Sutton of Leek landed on Gold Beach at noon on D-Day. *"I jumped into about three feet of water and waded on to the beach. We were stuck in a bomb crater for days living on hard biscuits and tinned food. I didn't have my clothes off for nine weeks,"* he said. Also going ashore on D-Day was Harry Stafford of Furness Vale who landed with No. 6 Bomb Disposal Section of the Royal Engineers.

Arthur Carrington of Chinley also served with a Royal Engineers unit and took part in the highly dangerous work of clearing unexploded bombs from Sheffield, Swansea and other blitzed cities. A Buxton man, Signalman Sam Pearson, was on board the sloop HMS Woodpecker in the Atlantic when she and two other warships sank U-264 in February 1944. Eleven of the U-boat's crew were rescued by the Woodpecker and Sam remembered seeing the German officers in his captain's cabin. A few days later the Woodpecker was sunk by another U-boat but, luckily, everyone on board, including Sam, was saved.

Able Seaman Billy Malkin of Station Street, Leek had two remarkable escapes. His ship was torpedoed in the Atlantic and he came to in the water holding on to a door. Months later he was torpedoed a second time and ingested a large amount of fuel oil. Then, in December 1943, the Hunt-class destroyer HMS Holcombe, on which he was now serving, was torpedoed and sunk by U-593 off Algeria. Billy Malkin was one of those rescued but he died from his injuries in hospital the next day.

There were unusual meetings. Royal Naval seaman Sam Lomas of Chapel-en-le-Frith recalled bumping into a friend from home - they had joined the Air Training Corps together in 1942 - in Colombo, Ceylon. He and Peter Clowes had been drafted to the same ship early in 1945 and they were soon exchanging local newspapers and letters from home.

Altogether it was a strange war for many. Luckily, most of the Peak District servicemen came through it comparatively unscathed.

Now almost obscured by trees this impressive war memorial commemorates the 15 men from the villages of Dethick, Lea and Holloway who died in the First World War - and the three men who died on active service in the 1939-1945 war

Chapter Thirteen
Saucepans for Victory

The drive to collect articles that could be recycled to help the war effort grew in intensity from 1940 onwards and salvage committees were established in many communities. In one week in May 1942 a vigorous salvage drive in Whaley Bridge yielded 33 tons of paper, rags, textiles, scrap metal, rubber and bones, silver paper and even dog hair. All this was collected by 19 'street stewards'.

Kitchen waste was collected, sterilized and fed to pigs. Touring lorries carried away tins, gramophone records, jars and bottles. What it was all used for the villagers of the Peak never knew.

Following a national appeal for aluminium by the Minister of Aircraft Production in the dark days of 1940 a receiving depot for articles made wholly or partly of aluminium was set up in a double-fronted shop in Spring Gardens, Buxton. Mrs C. Newton Pratt, leader of the local Women's Voluntary Service, was in charge.

Soon the shop was full of kettles, saucepans, frying pans, colanders, hot-water bottles, cream jugs, pepper pots, hair curlers, spectacle cases and even a gramophone horn and an imitation diamond ring. *"The response has been marvellous,"* said Mrs Pratt.

A typical poster on display in the Peak District at this time read: *"2,000 aluminium saucepans make one aeroplane"*. Lord Beaverbrook said the need was urgent. The Royal Family stripped the kitchens of Buckingham Palace and the War Office managed to find 500 tons of saucepans. But much of the aluminium salvaged was low-grade material quite unsuitable for the manufacture of fighter planes. In any case, it was pointed out that while housewives were being pestered to part with their pans large stocks of aluminium in scrap yards were not being claimed.

A vast amount of voluntary work was carried out by the WVS. These splendid ladies who wore green tweed suits with grey woven into them, beetroot-red jumpers and felt hats, received no payment and had to provide their uniforms with their own clothing coupons. They knitted and darned socks, served food and collected books, games and clothing to be sent to the forces. Their work was invaluable.

The rationing of food caused endless trouble, although it must be said that the nation's health was surprisingly good during the war. Inf ant mortality declined and the average age of death from natural causes increased. Ration books which had to include the names and addresses of retailers were issued. The basic weekly ration was fixed at 4oz of bacon, 2oz of tea, 8oz of sugar, 1 lb of meat, 8 oz of fats, 3 oz of cheese and two pints of milk. Tinned food on a points system became available from time to time.

"We had to send all redeemed coupons to the Food Office," said shopkeeper Marie Burton of Peak Dale. *"It was quite a job. One day I opened a box of them*

"Dig for Victory" became a popular slogan and a catchphrase that is still used today. This was a typical poster of the 1940s, its aim being to encourage the growing of produce in gardens and allotments

Posters like this seemed to be on every street corner during the war years. The collection of any form of paper was given top priority

An aluminium pile in 1940

to find to my horror that mice had chewed them into little pieces. I emptied the pieces - it was just like confetti - into a large envelope and sent them off. To my surprise it worked - my allowance of rationed food came through as usual."

A total of 48 clothing coupons for one year stretched individuals' ingenuity. A man's suit would take 24 coupons, woollen frocks 11 coupons and a pair of kid shoes 9 coupons. Cotton sheets were unobtainable unless you had just been married or bombed out. But cigarettes and cosmetics were not rationed.

One Derbyshire woman who got married in 1940 went on honeymoon wearing a blue coat her clever mother had made for her. She could not afford a hat so wore a piece of cloth in the shape of a turban. *"By the end of the war we all hated those turbans and scarves,"* she said. Another young wife living in the Peak fed her baby

"Don't waste food", the message in an advertisement that regularly appeared in Peak District newspapers.
A popular character was Potato Pete. People were urged to eat more potatoes at the height of the U-boat crisis

on cod liver oil, rose-hip syrup and poor-quality orange juice. No canned baby foods were available.

Tiered wedding cakes on reception tables would be artfully made of plaster of Paris. Inside these fake creations would be home-made sponge cake for guests to enjoy. Dame Barbara Cartland, the authoress who served in the Auxiliary Territorial Service during the war, wanted women in the forces to marry in *"the dress of their dreams"* and supplied 120 wedding dresses for hire at £1 a time.

People who exercised some influence in the community, perhaps well-to-do businessmen or farmers, would sometimes persuade shopkeepers in increase their ration entitlements. In Bakewell, for example, one particular farmer would roll out of the Peacock or the Anchor on Market Day, enter a grocer's shop and demand *"two pounds o' butter, four pounds o' sugar, two pounds o' cheese, a pound o' tea and four ounces o' twist."* But the grocer sometimes saw the man approaching and swiftly locked his door.

Those people who kept hens in their back gardens were able to trade surplus eggs for tea and sugar. At a charity auction in Bakewell in 1944 the Marquis of Hartington's wife, Kathleen Kennedy, wearing a Red Cross uniform, auctioned chickens from Chatsworth and laughingly posed with one bird tucked under her arm.

Petrol was strictly rationed. Its price was fixed in 1939 at 1s 6d a gallon and after March 1942 only essential users could fill the tanks of their vehicles. Farmer Donald Morten of Cowdale mixed paraffin with the petrol in the tank of his car. *"It used to smoke like fury, but it worked,"* he said.

Children bemoaned the meagre allowance of chocolates and sweets. Just 12 ounces were allowed each month, the chocolate arriving at the shops in large blocks. At Edensor *"it was broken into pieces with a hammer,"* recalled Nancie Park. At Wirksworth paper twists of sherbet could be purchased for a shilling at Miss Reece's shop in North End. No coupons were needed for a sweetened powder called "kayli" at a stall in the

Housewives were the target of most salvage appeals. The Ministry of Supply was responsible for this notice which appeared in national and local newspapers

town's Tuesday market.

In Chesterfield, Glossop, Matlock and other towns the Government opened British Restaurants so that women could escape from cooking chores and give more time to war work. Despite opposition from private cafe and restaurant owners more than 2,000 of these popular places, offering cheap meals between noon and 2 pm, had been opened across the country by September 1943. The main dish cost 6d, a pudding only 2d and tea 1d. At Wirksworth, for example, diners bought vouchers at the entrance and exchanged them for dishes of their choice. Max Hodnett remembered that spam and semolina pudding often seemed to be on the menu. Joan Hambleton recalled *"a good dinner and a pudding for a shilling"* at the British Restaurant in Regent Street, Leek.

The Ministry of Food was desperate to conserve vital foodstuffs in case the peril from U-boats reached unsupportable levels. As a consequence secret food depots were established in various parts of the Peak. Riber Castle on the hills overlooking Matlock was requisitioned as an emergency food depot. In Wildboarclough part of Crag Mill, where carpets for the 1851 Great Exhibition were once printed, was used to store food, and vital supples of tinned fruit and boxes of flour shared two floors of Clough Mill in Little Hayfield with the blocks of soap and bundles of candles that were manufactured there.

Many people in the Peak District responded when a Government "Grow More Food" campaign was launched in a radio broadcast in October 1939. All able-bodied men and women were urged to dig allotments in their spare time. The phrase "Dig for Victory" became a catchy slogan. Allotment societies were encouraged to buy seed and fertilizer in bulk and sell it on to gardeners at cost price. When an "Eat More Potatoes" campaign was introduced in 1940 the consumption of "spuds" rose by a massive 60% in Britain.

Some allotments led to unexpected problems, however. Jim Barrett kept a few hens in a shed on his small allotment at Peak Dale to eke out the egg ration. Youngsters raided the shed and carried away several eggs one evening, only to find that they were pot ones - Jim's hens had gone "broody." Yes, wartime life could sometimes be embarrassing, even for thieves.

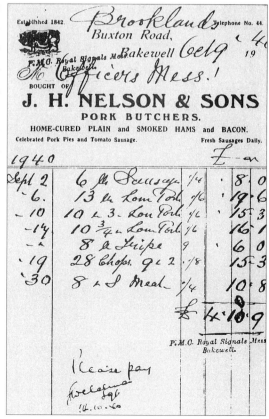

A bill to the Officers' Mess of the Royal Signals

So many railway workers joined the armed forces that local women were recruited as cleaners at the Rowsley engine sheds. Here 17 of them pose with shift foreman Jack Hibbs in the early 1940s.

Wagons loaded with large batteries destined for the Royal Navy's fleet of submarines were often seen in the sidings at Bakewell Station. The batteries were manufactured in the D.P. works at nearby Lumford Mill

Chapter Fourteen
Goats on the Platform

The bulk of war traffic was carried by rail and the extra loads put tremendous strain on locomotives and rolling stock. Many workshops, where equipment was regularly overhauled, were switched to munitions production and by the end of 1943 nearly 500 antiquated locomotives which in peacetime would have been scrapped were still puffing around the countryside. The situation nationally was so bad that in the winter of 1942 trains were being cancelled at the rate of 1,000 a week. Yet goods traffic had risen by 50 per cent .

There were usually no restaurant cars on passenger trains and the corridors of coaches were packed with servicemen going on leave or transferred war workers crossing the country to rejoin their families.

Blue-coated bulbs of low wattage were fitted in carriages, making reading difficult at night, and blinds drawn to prevent enemy aircraft spotting moving trains. The writer Vera Brittain grumbled: *"Before nightfall the blinds are drawn down and the railway carriage, if lighted at all, is illumined by a blue pin-point of light not strong enough to enable me to distinguish the features in the pale ovals which are my neighbours' faces."*

Members of the forces stepping out on to the platform at Matlock or Bakewell were sometimes surprised to find women in porters' uniforms hauling trolleys heaped with luggage or milk churns. Many women, in fact, took over men's jobs on the railways. A woman porter at Buxworth managed to combine her part-time job at the village station with running a corset-fitting service at her nearby home.

One Peak District woman who was a music teacher moved to the railway works at Derby to be trained as a blacksmith. She discovered that two of her colleagues formerly worked in a greengrocery shop and a wine shop.

A Charlesworth woman was conscripted to work in a signal box on the LNER line near Glossop. *"It was a very lonely life,"* she said. *"We often had to work 12 hour shifts, alternate days and nights. There was a small air raid shelter inside the box and the windows were taped to stop flying glass in the event of an explosion. We had a paraffin lamp over the desk with a tin shade so that we could record trains passing the box."*

One of two railway lorries used to carry goods from Bakewell Station to outlying addresses, a 30-cwt Dennis, was driven by Jessica, a local woman whom many people remembered as being particularly attractive and smartly dressed. A less glamorous role was carried out by 17 women at Rowsley engine sheds. They were recruited as locomotive cleaners on shift work and had to wear oil-stained overalls to clamber under the wheels of grimy steam locomotives in the sidings.

The senior ticket clerk at Chapel-en-le-Frith Station on the Midland line was

You must put the STING in the MOSQUITO!

BRITISH Railways are carrying supplies to war fronts all over the world and to war factories all over Britain.

This is the biggest battle of supplies any nation's Railways have ever had to fight — and you are in it.

By staying at home and leaving the Railways free for war transport, you can put the sting in the Mosquito and directly strike a blow for Victory.

RAILWAY EXECUTIVE COMMITTEE

To ease congestion on the railways people were advised to stay at home. This poster was issued by the Railway Executive, a forerunner of British Railways which came in after the War

Lily Bennett who handled wages for all railwaymen from Peak Forest to New Mills and supervised the accounts of local customers. *"I sometimes cycled in the blackout - a paper screening my lamp shining on the front wheel - to the Ferodo works. They despatched three trolley loads of brake linings from the station each day but they were slow to pay their account."* On one occasion the diligent Mrs Bennett accosted Ferodo's chief accountant and accompanied him to the bank to ensure that the railway received an overdue payment.

Wage packets for railwaymen at Gowhole sidings or the big station at Chinley were placed inside a leather bag and sent by rail in the hands of porter Adam Money, stationmaster George Clough escorting him solemnly from the ticket office and along the platform to the waiting train.

Another porter at this busy station was Tom, a 70 year-old veteran of the First World War who had proudly retained his army boots from 1918. He and Mrs Bennett were called upon to weigh a batch of goats which were being sent from a local farm to Surrey on the 8.28 pm train to Derby. *"The smell was terrible,"* said Mrs Bennett. *"Tom slapped tickets on each animal and tethered them to a couple of platform trolleys in a small store room at the end of the platform. But when the 8.28 arrived we found that the goats had eaten all the tickets and labels. The train's guard, Tom Shirt, protested at the absence of tickets and refused to take them."*

On another day a ram arrived for Barrett's farm. The station staff would not go near it but signalman Sam Bacon eventually dragged it to his box and tied it up until it was collected. Another farmer who paid about £200 a month for cattle to be transported by rail, always paid promptly with bundles of crumpled £5 notes.

Mrs Bennett remembered the manager of Lipton's, a local grocery store, complaining that a carton of cakes delivered by rail had been tampered with. Inquiries were instantly made by stationmaster Clough and he soon found an incriminating knife in the goods department which had been used to cut several slabs of Dundee cake. Men in the department had been helping themselves.

Chapel-en-le-Frith Central Station. The signalbox to which Sam Bacon once tethered a ram is no longer there. Trains stopped calling here in 1968

Apologies were made to Lipton's but the culprits were never caught .

At the height of the German invasion of Russia in 1941 a train loaded with tanks rattled through Chapel Station. Young porter Jim Morrison, who cycled each day from Edale, said: *"I'll drive one of those to Tomsk one day."* A few months later he joined the army and achieved his ambition of becoming a tank driver.

An American troop train stopped in the station one day in 1943 and a soldier handed Mrs Bennett a Persian kitten. *"Where he got it from I've no idea,"* she said. *"But I took it home and it was a lovely little thing."*

Inevitably, there was trouble on the line occasionally. A heavy Birmingham-bound train loaded with ammunition and being hauled over the steeply-graded Peak line by two locomotives snapped its couplings at Peak Forest in 1944. The train, without its engines, ran backwards through Dove Holes Tunnel and Chapel Station but was swiftly diverted on to the Hope Valley line and after travelling more than five miles came to a halt safely on a rising gradient near Cowburn Tunnel. If a signalman at Chinley South Junction, high above the great viaducts at Chapel Milton, had not acted so decisively the consequences could have been catastrophic.

Another coupling failure caused an accident in the same area in 1945. Thirty-six wagons ran away from Peak Forest, hit a set of catch points at the mouth of Dove Holes Tunnel and piled up in a gigantic heap of splintered wood and twisted steel. Driver Jack Merrett recalled: *"There were lamb carcasses and tea chests scattered everywhere. Tea was rationed and we were told to help ourselves. I filled the pockets of my overalls until I was loaded down. One driver got a leg of lamb from the carnage and cooked it on his shovel in his engine's firebox. But I can't say I enjoyed it very much."* Lamb on the shovel? That was certainly a dish unfamiliar to the harassed housewives of the Peak.

Torr Vale Mill lies deep in a gorge of the River Goyt at New Mills. An ENSA concert in 1941 was a great success. The mill was on essential war work, turning out material for army and air force uniforms

Below: Going to the pictures was a favourite habit for thousands of people in the Peak during the war. A queue is seen outside the Cinema at Wirksworth one day in 1941. The film might have been Gone With the Wind.

Chapter Fifteen
'Rose Marie" at the Mill

Early one afternoon in May 1941 the soothing sound of a woman singing the Indian Love Call from Rose Marie floated out of the windows of Torr Vale Mill at New Mills. The sun was shining and the song, amplified through a microphone, could be heard by shoppers in Union Road high above the gorge in which the mill still stands.

ENSA - the Entertainments National Service Association - had come to town and a party of professional stage artistes was presenting a show for several hundred women and girls, and some of their relatives, who had gathered in the weaving mill's freshly-decorated canteen for their lunchtime break.

At that period of the war many concert parties were touring the country to put on shows once and sometimes twice a day at munitions works and other factories that were employed on national service. In the previous week alone they had staged 101 shows and ENSA was hoping to exceed that number the following week. All that factory managements had to do was provide transport and give the artistes a meal before they moved on to the next works.

The women who vacated their looms at W.S. Lowe and Sons' five-storey mill were delighted when Mr Harry Bullough their manager informed them that Harry Young's concert party was on its way. There were no speeches of introduction and no votes of thanks. Time was too precious and the cloth the women produced was urgently needed for military uniforms.

The Rose Marie musical number was contributed by the soprano Doris Ingham and she was followed on to the mill's makeshift stage by Edward Ellis with his farmyard imitations, the comedienne Irene Williams who impersonated Will Fyfe and Shirley Temple, and Rene Young (described as "radio's youngest accordionist") who had the audience singing loudly and returning to work with their own deafening rendition of *"There'll Always be an England"* ringing in their ears.

ENSA had been formed early in 1940, its first broadcast being a dinner-hour show for factory workers at Woolwich Arsenal in July that year. The Minister of Labour, Ernest Bevin, was in the audience.

As the war progressed other factories in the Peak received visits from concert parties similar to the group that visited New Mills. Workers' Playtime, in fact, became a popular radio programme. Roy Hudd, the comedian and actor, made his debut in such a broadcast from the canteen of the Ferodo factory in Chapel-en-le-Frith in 1944. *"Jimmy Clitheroe topped the bill,"* he recalled. *"We got £7.l0s for the broadcast and £2.l0s subsistence. I made a profit because I only paid £l.l0s for bed and breakfast in Chapel."*

Radio, or wireless as it was then usually called, provided staple entertainment for most people during the war. Henry Hall playing *Here's to the Next Time*, Arthur

Askey in Bandwagon, Larry the Lamb on Children's Hour, Jack Warner presiding over Garrison Theatre, Charles Shadwell and his Orchestra, Monday Night at Eight, the irrepressible Tommy Handley in ITMA and, most frequently of all, Sandy Macpherson at the BBC theatre organ.

The cinema attracted thousands of Peak District people each week. There would be two shows each night, and usually matinees on Saturdays, at the Cinema and Art Theatre in New Mills, the Princes Palace in Whaley Bridge, the Opera House and Spa in Buxton, the Grand and Majestic in Leek, the Empire in Glossop, the Ritz, Palace and Cinema House in Matlock, the Cinema in Wirksworth and the Picture House in Bakewell, for example. Admission prices ranged from 3d to 1s.

Harry Berrisford, who often travelled by bus from Dove Holes to see films at the Spa Cinema in Buxton, said: "The two-hour programmes usually started with a short 'interest' film which might show the manufacture of shovels or the life of a glass-blower. This could be followed by an equally short film - Buster Keaton chased by scores of policemen or Tommy Trinder wisecracking at the camera - and then came a Ministry of Information shortie 'Safeguard children against diphtheria', 'Save your waste' or 'Eat more potatoes'".

A typical programme would also include a Gaumont-British, Universal or Paramount newsreel with graphic pictures of Malta convoys under attack, the King

inspecting army cadets "somewhere in England" and bombs exploding on the Russian front. There might be a Donald Duck or Pluto cartoon and then the main feature - Broadway Melody, Moon Over Burma, Lost Horizon. All in black and white. There was an added bonus if the film was in colour.

But the two hours of magic did not always run smoothly. At the Empress Cinema in Chapel-en-le-Frith there were occasions when the film came to an abrupt halt. Sidney Liversidge, on leave from the army, remembered the screen going blank and a loud hum booming from the loudspeakers. *"We whistled, shouted and stamped our feet,"* he said. *"After some time Mr Fletcher, the projectionist, could be seen rushing into his box and the film would continue."*

Posters like this drew attention to concerts by ENSA at munitions factories throughout the land

When air raid sirens sounded audiences were usually given a warning, a message being flashed on to the screen or a brief announcement made by the cinema manager. On one such occasion at the Buxton Opera House the manager, Captain F.S. Holmes, appeared on the stage with a hand torch and said *"Ladies and gentlemen."* Then he fell into the orchestra pit amid much laughter. He was unhurt despite his loss of dignity.

At the town's rival cinema, the Spa in Spring Gardens, manager Bob Parker drove into Manchester during the 1940 blitz in a determined bid to obtain the latest Hollywood films for his patrons.

Villagers around Bakewell travelled in by bus to see films at the Picture House. When the Turner family went to see Mrs Miniver they emerged from the cinema to find that the last bus home had departed - no one had told the driver that the film ran 30 minutes longer than usual. *"We were now faced with a seven-mile walk to Eyam,"* said David Turner. About 30 people had missed the bus and heavy rain meant they were soaked before reaching home.

The Ministry of Information organised a fleet of mobile cinema units to tour the country. A 16mm projector would be set up on a table in the Mechanics' Institute at Eyam or the Town Hall at Chapel-en-le-Frith and propaganda films projected on to a portable screen. Sometimes the films were shown in a van parked in the market place at Wirksworth or Ashbourne, a small screen at the rear of the vehicle being shaded by shutters. *"In sunlight it was usually very difficult to see what was going on,"* recalled one observer. *"In any case, the films were often old newsreels or short films giving advice on gardening or kitchen recipes."*

Despite the blackout, locally organised events were always guaranteed to attract packed audiences. The Married Ladies' Fellowship of Chinley Independent Chapel co-opted their sons and daughters to prepare colourful posters for display in shop windows in the weeks preceding their annual concert. The audience would gather in the Wash Road Sunday School, sitting on rows of bare wooden benches, and applaud *The Dentist,* an act on the school platform that was always a sure-fire hit. In this sketch local farmer Heskey Higginbottom and several hefty lads removed a patient's enormous tooth with a huge rope that could have moored the Queen Mary.

This was followed by members of the Chapel-en-le-Frith Male Voice Choir clambering on to the stage. The choir had been founded in 1918 by young men returning from the First World War and though its strength was depleted it still maintained its tradition during World War II. The men's rendition of *Comrades in Arms* and *The Jolly Roger,* with conductor Tom Longson waving his arms energetically, invariably produced a storm of applause.

Me and the Moke and Liza was a duet, one of the married ladies playing a violin, the other wearing her husband's flat cap and grey flannel trousers. Members of the audience, many of them farmers and their wives who recognised their neighbours on the stage, thought this was hilarious. Village life has certainly not been the same since the Married Ladies' Concert was abandoned many years ago.

Parties of school children from the Peak District were taken to Buxton to see the Old Vic Theatre Company when they made a provincial tour in 1940 subsidised by the Government. Well-known actors including Renee Asherson, Alec Clunes and Sonia Dresdel appeared at the Opera House in *Twelfth Night* and *She Stoops to Conquer*. Later there were performances of *The Marriage of Figaro* and *La Traviata* by the Sadlers Wells touring company and a concert by the London Symphony Orchestra.

Inspired perhaps by these stage productions the evacuated girls of Westcliff High School put on two short plays, *Fat King Melon* and *The Dumb Wife of Cheapside*, at the Constitution Hall in Chapel-en-le-Frith at the end of the autumn term in 1941. The school rented the hall, sold every seat on two nights and handed over all proceeds to the local Red Cross and the Armed Forces' Comforts Fund.

"The evenings were very successful and reflected much credit on Miss Helmore, the teacher who produced the plays," said Miss Wilkinson, the headmistress. *"In this way the school was able to repay some of the debt it owed to the people of Chapel-en-leFrith."* The school's music mistress, Miss K. Murphy, later organised a production of Merrie England in the Constitution Hall. *"Everyone in the audience joined in the singing and it was marvellous,"* commented fellow teacher Miss Alice Hughes.

Ballroom dancing - and "jiving" when American troops arrived in Britain in 1942 - was another popular leisure activity and the Peak District spawned many small dance bands. There was often a shortage of male participants due to the absence of young men in the services and girls were obliged to dance together. Dances were usually in aid of comforts funds, the Red Cross Parcels Fund, Aid to Russia, the Spitfire Fund or some other worthy and patriotic cause.

Ron Farrell, a local man who played the organ at the parish church on Sundays, formed a band to play for mid-week dances at the Town Hall in Wirksworth. Dances at the Drill Hall near Matlock Green also attracted youngsters from far and wide - a late bus being laid on for Wirksworth and Bonsall "jitterbuggers". Jim Fox and his band catered for dancers at the Women's Institute in Chinley, arranging spot prizes, progressive old-time numbers and excuse-me quicksteps, the evenings closing with a dreamy "last waltz."

Big bands that were frequently heard on the radio, Ted Heath, Joe Loss, Billy Ternent and Oscar Rabin, for example, turned up from time to time in the Pavilion Gardens at Buxton or the Matlock Bath Pavilion.

As an alternative to dancing the entertainment seekers of the Peak would travel by train to see pantomimes in the nearby big cities. At Christmas in 1940 Pat Kirkwood starred in Cinderella at the Princes Theatre and Tessie O'Shea in The Sleeping Beauty at the Palace in Manchester while Frank Randle appeared as

Aladdin at the Lyceum in Sheffield.

Travelling fairs managed to obtain sufficient fuel to bring their tractors and vans to villages of the Peak throughout the war. Gigantic Steam Yachts "Shamrock" and "Columbia" that swung to and fro either side of a powerful traction engine formed the main feature of Waddington's Fair in the late 1930s and early 1940s.

Clifford Bowen remembered the fair that pitched camp at the bottom of Union Road in New Mills. "We had to go during daytime in the holidays," he said. "I suppose the blackout snuffed out most of the fairy lights at night." Showman Mark Walker, who supervised the stalls from a spick-and-span gas-lit caravan, confirmed that the roundabout lights were "subdued" each evening.

Oakley's Fair, erected each year on land behind the Miners Arms in Eyam, attracted youngsters to the Noah's Ark roundabout with its glittering array of wooden cockerels, tigers, horses and unicorns on which were fitted velvet-covered seats. Noah's Ark also featured in Hibbert's Fair which toured the northern townships and villages of the Peak. At Whitsuntide in 1940 and 1941 fairground attractions were set up in a field next to Burton's Farm in Beech Lane, Dove Holes, with Arthur Hibbert, wearing a cloth cap, perched at a pay desk in a small cabin at the side of the "dobby horses" roundabout. There were rolling-penny stalls, coconut shies, swing boats and donkey rides along the lane. On many evenings Mr Hibbert would walk from his caravan to sit with Dick Burton on a stone bench outside the farmhouse door and chat amiably over a pipe of baccy. After three days the fair moved on to Fairfield Common at Buxton.

From time to time small travelling circuses pitched camp in the Peak. One was Rosario's which erected its red-and-white striped "big top" in a field near Chapel-en-le-Frith's cricket ground. For an extra 3d visitors could view a menagerie which consisted of a few cages on wheels. Roy Hill, then a 15-year-old schoolboy, remembered seeing the animals in 1941. *"In one cage was a large placid-looking rodent"*, he said. *"A card on the bars described it as 'The world's biggest rat - caught in a Berlin sewer'. In later years, however, I realised that it was in fact a harmless South American coypu."*

Another small circus that visited several sites in the Peak was Paulo's which attracted crowds of children when its "big top" went up. This family circus was formed by Clara Paulo and the star attraction was her daughter who performed tricks in the ring, such as leaping through a paper hoop, while on horseback.

Women were particularly active in the organisation of social events during the war. They had to be, of course. The Married Ladies at Chinley Chapel met each Wednesday afternoon to knit socks for the forces. "One of our members, Mrs Hughie Hughes from The Breck, a leading light in the Women's Voluntary Service, was able to obtain wool for us," said Alice Clowes.

At Eyam whist drives in the Mechanics' Institute were popular, as they were at many other villages. The broadcaster, the Reverend G. Bramwell Evens, well-known as "Romany", visited Edale and Chinley to give an open-air illustrated talk on birds to Scouts and Guides. Foden's works band, with its renowned cornet player Harry Mortimer, filled the Empress Cinema when they gave a concert for the Chapel-en-le-Frith comforts fund in 1942.

A ladies' cricket team took the field at Chapel in the summer of 1942, leading players being Connie Pink, the captain, and Marion Bagshawe who lived at Ford Hall. Outdoor swimming pools at Park Hall, Little Hayfield, at Roeside near Chapel-en-le-Frith and at Waterswallows near Buxton, all attracted crowds during the hot summers of 1940 and 1941, but eventually closed to everyone's regret.

Church bells had been silenced since the start of the war. Only the military or the police were authorised to sound the bells to give warning of an "invasion". But when General Montgomery's 8th Army put the Germans into full retreat at the Battle of El Alamein the Government allowed all the country's churches to ring their bells in celebration. *"This is not the end,"* said Winston Churchill. *"It is not even the beginning of the end. But it is, perhaps, the end of the beginning."*

The sound of the bells ringing across the countryside made everyone feel brighter and gave them the confidence that victory was at last on its way. Mrs Cissy Bamford walked to church in Chapel Milton on Sunday November 15th 1942 and looked up in disbelief when the building's old Victorian bell began to clang high in its tower. *"The 15-year-old son of a friend of mine had been called out by the minister, Mr Powicke, and the lad looked very proud of his role on that historic day,"* she said.

El Alamein paved the way for the Allied march to victory and when peace in Europe eventually arrived in May 1945 flags appeared in windows throughout the Peak. *"Wirksworth went wild,"* said Max Hodnett. *"There was dancing in the street outside the cinema. Someone brought a gramophone and rigged up a loudspeaker. Everyone seemed to be there."* A large Union Jack hung outside Edensor Church and despite persistent rain a large bonfire was lit on Bunker's Hill at Chatsworth. Many people thought it rather appropriate that German prisoners-of-war had been recruited to clear away brushwood for the crowd that gathered. A dummy of Hitler was thrown on the flames.

The bells of the floodlit St Edward's Parish Church in Leek rang out all afternoon and at dusk large crowds gathered. There was dancing in Derby Street and a large bonfire flared up in Chorley Street. Many people went to the parish church for a service of thanksgiving in the evening led by the Reverend N.W. Martin. Teas and games for children were organised at short notice in many villages and at Rowsley the British Legion paraded in Peacock Square.

The five bells high in the tower of Ilam Church chimed over the Manifold Valley and in Chinley Alice Clowes wrote in her diary: *"Church bells rang today, there were fireworks going off everywhere and we put a flag up."* Then she went to

The front page of the Daily Mail on May 8 1945 says it all. Crowds gathered through the land

church and wrote a letter to her son who was serving in the Royal Navy. *"Thank God it's almost all over,"* she wrote.

But it would be another three months before the war against Japan concluded. Nevertheless, victory in Europe lifted a great yoke from the citizens of Britain. The Peak District had come through the six-year ordeal with flying colours. It had escaped much of the mayhem and tragedy that afflicted more populous areas of the country. It had suffered and survived. The scarlet skies over the hills of the Peak had given way to bright sunshine and the promise of what many people hoped would be a new age.

Dried egg, introduced in 1941, typified war time diet

FOR FURTHER READING

ASHBOURNE NEWS TELEGRAPH.

ATKINSON, BARBARA: The Home Front (Tameside -Leisure Services, 1995).

BANKS, ARTHUR: Wings of the Dawning (Images Publishing, Malvern, 1996).

BOYLAN, MARSHALL S.: A Moorlands Dedication (William Beech, Leek, 1992).

BRICKHILL, PAUL: The Dambusters (Evans Brothers, London, 1951).

BUXTON ADVERTISER.

BYFORD, JAMES S.: Moorland Heritage.

CALDER, ANGUS: The People's War (Jonathan Cape, London, 1969).

COLLIER, RON: Dark Peak Aircraft Wrecks (Leo Cooper, London, 1995).

DAVIE, MICHAEL: The Diaries of Evelyn Waugh.

DAVIES, C. STELLA: North Country Bred.

DERBYSHIRE LIFE.

DEVONSHIRE, DUCHESS OF: The Estate (Macmillan, London, 1990).

FLETCHER, BARRY & BILL: A Bradwell Man (High Peak Books, Hathersage, 1998).

GAUKROGER, SUSAN & HOLLIDAY, JOYCE: Memoirs of the Moorland Farmer.

GIBSON, GUY: Enemy Coast Ahead (Michael Joseph, London, 1946).

GRAVES, JOHN: Jottings of a Staffordshire Parson's Son.

HALLAM, VIC: Silent Valley at War (Sheaf Publishing, Sheffield, 1990).

HIGH PEAK COURIER.

HIGH PEAK REPORTER.

HODGES, RICHARD: Wall-to-Wall History - Story of Roystone Grange (Duckworth, London, 1991)

HODNETT, MAX: A Wirksworth Boyhood 1941-1958 (Happy Walking, Matlock,

HUDSON, BILL: Through Limestone Hills (Oxford Publishing, 1989).

LAURIE, KEDRUN: Cricketer Preferred (Lyme Park, 1979).

LEEK & DISTRICT HISTORICAL SOCIETY: Leek at War.

LEWIS, STEPHEN: A Debt of Honour (S,P, Lewis, New Mills, 1999).

MERRETT, JACK: Peak District Railwayman (Old Mill Books, Little Eaton, 1989).

MORTEN, J. R. D.: The Trivial Round - the Common Touch.

NICHOLSON, JENNY: Where Heather Blooms on Ladylow (Church in Market Place, Buxton, 2000)

PARK, NANCIE: Schooldays at Chatsworth (Derbyshire Countryside, Derby, 1994).

PEAK ADVERTISER .

PEAK TIMES .

PORTEUS, CRICHTON: Changing Valley (Michael Joseph, london, 1950).

SHELDON, C ,W,: In Name Only (Three Counties, Leek, 2000) .

SMITH, PETER, J.C.: Flying Bombs over the Pennines.

TEMPEST, ANNE: Baslow 2000.

SWEETMAN, JOHN: The Dambusters' Raid .

TURNER, DAVID: A Tyke in Tupland (David Turner, Sheffield, 2000) .

VIRTUE, ALAN: Memoirs of a Derbyshire Hill Farmer.

WESTSIDE MAGAZINE .

WHITEHEAD, RON: Rowsley 1849-1999.

WOMEN'S INSTITUTES: Derbyshire Within Living Memory (Countryside Books, 1996) .

WOMEN'S INSTITUTES: The Derbyshire Village Book (Countryside Books, 1991).

INDEX